What people are saying about *Dashboard Bagels: Dishing Up Food for Thought*

Knowing Lance professionally as a clerk of the federal court, I found his book easy to read, and full of unique stories. His perspective of life's ebbs and flows kept me anticipating with interest the next chapter of *Dashboard Bagels.*

—U.S. Senator Harry Reid (Ret.)

Dashboard Bagels is a fine book that is filled with good stories and advice. The author, Lance Wilson, completed a splendid career as a nationally recognized state and federal court administrator before becoming an author. This easy-to-read book has a food theme. Each chapter begins with a "food quote" and ends with "recipe reminders." He reflects on his experiences that taught him lessons about life, morality, and common sense. He quotes famous people (e.g., "Cooking is one failure after another, and that's how you finally learn" - Julia Child) and even gets Elvis Presley into the act. I highly recommend this book, especially for those in leadership positions.

—William K. Suter
Major General, JAGC, USA (Ret.)
Clerk of the U.S. Supreme Court (Ret.)

What a wonderful series of stories. Inspirational, funny, thoughtful, and sure to make you smile. Lance is both a talented artist and engaging writer. A book for all ages, this is a collection of stories and illustrations you just want to curl up by a warm fire and read.

—Scott Cohen, Artist & Playwright
Life Cube Project

What I loved about *Dashboard Bagels* was the profound insights in to the complexities of daily life. I was moved by how observations from seemingly routine interactions brought unexpected inspiration. Keeping the "recipe reminders" from each chapter in mind when I find myself in similar situations helps me stay positive and to always look for the best in people. Dashboard Bagels helped me to see the beauty in everyday life.

—The Honorable Nancy Allf
Eighth Judicial District, Clark County

A light hearted, thought provoking reminder about life and how we choose to live.

—Terri Janison, President & CEO
Grant a Gift, Autism Foundation

The author takes a unique and humorous approach to sharing his positive life lessons. Read *Dashboard Bagels* front to back or crack it open in the middle- either way you'll find helpful tips to apply in your own life!

—Keely Brooks, President
Southern Nevada Bicycle Association

If you like to make your own dumb mistakes, don't read this book! If you like the wisdom of experience wrapped in good stories, do read this book! Lance welcomes the reader in true, honest and heartfelt glimpses of a life well lived.

—Pastor David Krueger-Duncan (ret.)

Fill up on the life lessons in *Dashboard Bagels*. The personal experiences and thought-provoking stories will nourish your mind and spirit.

— Michelle Zellner,
Author of *The You Revolution: The Journey of a Better Being*

A thoughtful series of life examples through real stories. The Judge Roll / Gabriella Giffords story was especially powerful. The culinary quotes, pedaling proverbs, and disconnecting the dots makes this a unique book for navigating the complex world in which we live. The easy to read summaries and bullet points make this book easy to apply to everyday life. I recommend this book without reservation. Thanks Lance!

—Johnathan Edwards, M.D.
Author of Chasing Dakar
Doc Edwards Fitness Sports & Wellness.
Docedwardsfitness.com

Dashboard Bagels is a delicious smorgasbord for the mind. It's the perfect mental snack for the curious mind, made up of simple recipes and real life scenarios. My two favorite ingredients are from chapter 16, curiosity and humility, which make for an exciting, never boring, always learning and growing life. Lance Wilson is not afraid to tell it like it is with refreshing, untainted honesty, and charming vulnerability as he brings personality to the page and victory to the challenges of everyday life. *Dashboard Bagels* is the friend you have not yet met, as the author describes his wife's view on strangers.

—Heather Fisher, President
Save Red Rock
Escape Adventures
Las Vegas Cyclery

Dashboard Bagels:
Dishing Up Food for Thought

Inspirational Stories
Lance Wilson

Lance Wilson

Copyright © 2019 Lance Wilson

ISBN – 9781734140309 (Paperback Edition)
ISBN – 9781734140316 (E-Book Edition)

Author Statement: I have done my best to recreate events from my memories. While I believe these stories are reported accurately, should someone have firsthand experience of one of these events which differs from the way I portrayed it, I would be pleased to hear from that person. Also, every effort has been made to trace or contact all copyright holders. I will be pleased to make good any omissions or rectify any mistakes brought to my attention. Please contact me at dashboardbagels@gmail.com

Library of Congress Control Number – 2019917879

Printed and Bound in the United States of America - First printing, 2019.

Cover Illustration and Book Layout and Design by Brian Swanson - www.brianswansonstudio.com

Author photograph by Steve Patchin - www.patchinpictures.com

Published By –   Lance Wilson
                 Las Vegas, NV

Dedicated to my mother, Kathleen Y. Wilson

A woman of vast intellect, curiosity, strength, and courage.

TABLE OF CONTENTS

PREFACE

"Recipes are important but only to a point. What's more important than recipes is how we think about food, and a good cookbook should open up a new way of doing that."

–Jacques Pepin

Like this quote from Jacques Pepin, French chef and television personality, *Dashboard Bagels* promises to open up new ways of thinking for you. While not a cookbook in the technical sense, a food theme is carried through this book by using food quotes at the beginning of each chapter and "Recipe Reminders" at the end of each chapter. This is done in the hope that *Dashboard Bagels* provides you with nourishment; that, like your favorite recipe, you come back to the lessons often and make them part of your life. I hope you savor them as much as you would a favorite meal.

Why did I write this book? One reason is my belief that the included stories are inspirational and morally significant. And I did not want to take these lessons to my grave –which is still hopefully a long way off! While the characters and situations in this book may be unique, I trust you have had equally interesting experiences. Please share these positive stories with your family, your friends, with strangers, and with the world. Why? Because I am convinced we can—and do—change the world for the better through the sharing of positive experiences. We are all too quick to broadcast the negative things we see and encounter. Yet we tend to stay mum about the many wonderful, loving events we encounter. When we share these experiences with others, they become part of the fabric of our world. They build on each other. They multiply exponentially. When we share love and hope, I believe two and two can equal six. As we share a smile, a positive thought, an uplifting story, it is contagious. Try it! You will make someone else smile and you will improve the world.

A second reason I wrote *Dashboard Bagels* is to pay homage to the people in these stories: men and women who have broadened my thinking, and who have dealt with challenging situations in constructive, uplifting ways. I am honored to have gotten to know all of those whose stories are included in this book, and I thank them for their strength and inspiration.

As my experiences influence my views on the included stories, a bit about my background may be helpful. I was born and raised in the beautiful farmland of Lancaster County, Pennsylvania. While my childhood had challenges (whose didn't?), I am blessed to have had a wonderfully supportive mother who did her best to raise two sons largely on her own. While far from wealthy, we always had a roof over our heads, food on the table, and, most importantly, unconditional love. Yes, I was truly blessed.

There was a huge emphasis on education in my home. I recall a childhood friend who practically grew up with our family and who my mother often referred to as her "third son" saying: "I am the only person in my family to have graduated from college. I attribute much of that to Mrs. Wilson. This is because her question was not *if* you were going to college but *where* you were going to college. It was just expected." I took this for granted until I heard my friend say this at my mother's funeral service.

I spent my professional career as an administrator in state and federal court systems. I was fortunate to move into leadership positions with the courts at a very early age, which is why you will see stories about judges and other court employees in this book. While our court systems are far from perfect, in my opinion they remain the best in the world. I feel honored to have had the privilege to work for our federal courts for most of my career. I also had a wide variety of jobs to put myself through college, including working as a garbage man, factory and foundry worker, security guard, farmhand, bill collector (sorry!), house painter, pizza maker, and dish washer. All of these experiences influenced my thinking.

My passions also undoubtedly come through in my writing. These include spending time with my family, riding bicycles, painting, swimming laps, playing with our dog Kya, and listening to jam band music. Curiosity and striving to be a lifelong learner are also passions of mine. I remain curious about what motivates us, why we do what we do, and why we make the choices we make. And, of course, I continue to learn from all with whom I come into contact.

Enjoy.

–Lance S. Wilson

Chapter 1

Chockie's Painting

"A recipe has no soul. You, as the cook, must bring soul to the recipe."

–Thomas Keller

I am sure you have heard this saying, or some variation of it: "If you love something, let it go. If it was meant to be yours, it will come back to you. If it does not come back, it was never yours in the first place." If you are a cynic, like I was before this story occurred, my reaction when hearing this statement was that it was a bunch of crock. But the travels of Chockie's Painting below is proof that loved objects and people can find their way back to you and, when they do, the outcome can be very powerful.

In my first year in college I became interested in painting and began exploring working in oils and acrylics. Eventually I decided that I wanted to try something harder, so I made my first attempt at using watercolors. For my first watercolor piece, I selected an image to paint based on a photograph in a *National Geographic* magazine. I essentially imitated the composition of the photo, as I was doing this as an exercise in learning the medium. (Note: If the original photographer sees this, please contact me, as I would love to give you proper credit for the composition.)

1

I named this painting "Chockie's Painting" after it took an interesting journey. Chockie was the moniker of a dear co-worker in my office. Her given name was Opal DeLoss Rector, but everyone called her Chockie. She never told me how this had become her nickname, and it remains a mystery to me to this day.

Chockie befriended me when I was working in my first professional position after graduate school. This friendship with Chockie developed while we both worked in the Court Administrator's Office in the Superior Court of Maricopa County in Phoenix, Arizona. We sat in neighboring workstations that were so close together that each of us could hear every word spoken by the other. Chockie was much older than me and had a great wisdom and insight. She was an accomplished sculptor, and we often had long, deep discussions during lunch or after work about art, spirituality, and life in general. I loved

2

chatting with her and exploring her views on these topics. Chockie provided a tremendous intellectual influence on my youthful life.

One day I brought my freshly painted watercolor into my work cubicle and hung it on one of the panels. It was visible to anyone who walked by, and it didn't go unnoticed by Chockie. I saw her staring at it several times.

After a few days Chockie approached me and told me how much she loved my watercolor. It was a very nice compliment to receive, especially from another artist. She marveled at the little boy pumping water so hard. For her, it demonstrated strength, determination, and an unwavering energy to overcome the challenge of filling the bucket.

Shortly thereafter, Chockie was diagnosed with cancer. She quickly became very ill and had to be hospitalized. When I heard about it, immediately I knew what I wanted to do. With hammer and nail in hand, I carted the painting to her hospital room and presented it to her as a gift. Checking the door to make sure the coast was clear, I hammered that nail right into the hospital wall and hung the painting directly across from Chockie's bed.

While touched by my gesture, Chockie refused to accept the painting because she knew it was my first attempt at watercolor. She also knew how much I liked the painting. But, given that she could not get out of bed, I flippantly told her it was not her decision; the painting was hanging in her room so it was hers! Still she persisted. After a bit of negotiation, we came to a compromise. She agreed to keep the painting "on loan," but stressed that I would always be its true owner. I said "Deal," and left it at that. Of course I had no intention of ever reclaiming the painting, but I kept that to myself.

Fortunately, Chockie recovered from this bout with cancer and returned to work. We continued to work side by side for a few more years until I transferred to another job. As often happens even with the best of friends, we lost touch with each other. Some 18 years later, I was preparing to display my artwork at a show and started reminiscing about the many paintings I had given away to friends over the years. I have never had any regrets about offering my paintings to others, but I did wish I had kept photos of them for my archives.

While reflecting on each of my long lost paintings, my mind flashed on Chockie. I had no idea what had happened to her. Given her past health challenges, I had a sinking feeling that she had passed away. Still, I decided to see if I could find her, both to reconnect and to ask her if I could take a photo of that inaugural watercolor for my portfolio.

I was living in Las Vegas at the time, and I guessed that Chockie was still in Phoenix if she was alive. I checked with some former co-workers who still worked in the office where she and I had become friends, but none of those people had any idea how to connect with her. So I took to my own research and, through the wonders of the Internet, I easily found an active phone number for Chockie in the Phoenix area and called right away.

It was wonderful to hear her voice after so many years. I will never forget her true delight with my surprise call. She said that I called just in time, because she was now in a hospice situation and very near death. Chockie shared that she had been thinking about me and worrying for months about how to get the painting back in my hands. She had asked several people if they knew where I was, but to no avail. She then stated how the little boy pumping water had given her strength, determination, and courage through her many years of health challenges. She asked for my address so she could mail the painting back to me. I was now on the opposite end of the protests. Just as she had objected to my hanging the painting in her hospital room many years before, I was now protesting her efforts to return the painting to me, despite the fact that this was our original agreement.

As it was only a short one-hour flight from Las Vegas to Phoenix, I decided to pay Chockie one last visit. I arrived, rented a car, and drove to her small home in an older part of the city. I walked up to her door with a certain level of anxiety, not knowing her condition or what to expect. It had been many years since we last saw each other.

All my anxiety disappeared immediately, thanks to a warm hug I received from her upon entering her bedroom. It was a somewhat awkward hug, as she could not get out of bed, but a great hug nonetheless. And, equally significant to the hug, I could see that her positive spirit was as strong as ever.

Chockie and I chatted about everything during that relatively short visit. She told me about having to retire from her position with the court due to her health challenges; I caught her up on my various career changes, the birth of my first son, and more. Of course we also talked about art and spirituality, the topics that had united us some 18 years earlier. Her energy level was not strong enough for me to stay very long. The hospice nurse ushered me out when she saw Chockie was tiring.

As I tried to depart without taking the painting, Chockie would have none of that! She reminded me again of our agreement and stressed that it was important for her to achieve closure in her life. The fear of leaving my painting orphaned was one less thing she needed to worry about as she prepared for her departure from this world. With tears streaming down my face, I reluctantly reclaimed the painting as I left her house and flew back to Las Vegas. On my way home, I noticed a large handwritten note taped to the back of the painting with my name on it. It was Chockie's request to whoever had the painting after she passed, stressing that they should try to find me to return since it "belonged" to me. It made me realize that she must have felt better giving the painting directly to me. She died only a few weeks later.

This painting now has a special place in my living room and in my heart. I experience waves of wonderful emotions each time I look at the little boy working so hard to use the pump larger than he is. I am constantly moved that something I created meant so much to another person for so long and helped her through her journey.

These events also ended my cynicism about the quote explained at the beginning of this story. I now had a concrete example of how something I loved could be released and then come back years later with a new and stronger meaning. Chockie was a prime example of an extraordinary person with incredible strength and compassion. While in her hospice situation, she did not worry about her impending death. Rather, her concern was how to find an old friend to return a painting to him.

"Chockie's Painting" will always have a special place in my heart, as will Chockie herself. Thank you, Chockie, for taking such good care of this painting for me for many years, for our friendship, and for all you have given to me and the world! And thank you for teaching me the value of letting go of something I love.

RECIPE REMINDERS FOR CHOCKIE'S PAINTING

- Do not hang onto things or people you love; share them with others and with the world. Stay in touch with current and old friends. We tend to underestimate the power of friendship and the connectivity we gain by such relationships.
- Develop a hobby. Find something you enjoy doing for the pure fun of doing, like painting.

Chapter 2

A Jerk of the Head Will Result in a Hat on the Sidewalk

"Don't be afraid to adapt new ingredients into your own techniques, and traditional ingredients into new recipes."

–Jose Garces

Early in my career as a court administrator, a professor from Arizona State University came to my office and asked if I could take a student of his as an intern. This was not a unique request, as the court regularly took on interns, and I truly loved the opportunity to help young people in their educational pursuits. The request began, as many others had, with the professor noting the student, Don Thompson, needed to do an internship in the field of criminal justice to complete the requirements for a Bachelor's degree in Criminal Justice. Just as I was about to say, "Of course, we'd love to have Don as an intern," the professor added an unexpected twist, announcing Don was a quadriplegic.

Many thoughts raced through my mind. While I wanted to help this young man, the challenges of doing this in the mid-1980s were numerous. We did not have the amazing automation enhancements we have today. We were still pushing stacks of paper around, as no one in the office even had a computer on

7

their desk. Wanting interns to have fruitful experiences, I had a hard time envisioning what Don could do to make his time with us productive for all involved. Thankfully the professor was insistent, singing Don's praises and pleading with me that someone had to give this young man a chance to prove himself. I agreed to accept Don as an intern. As you might expect me to say at this point, it turned out to be one of the best decisions of my working career. It was a powerful lesson in not letting limitations we think others may have keep us from taking a chance on them.

I recall vividly the first conversation I had with Don when he started his three-month internship with us in the Office of Court Administration in the Superior Court in Maricopa County, Arizona. He rolled into my office in his electric wheelchair and we initially exchanged pleasantries. Early in the discussion I was brutally candid with Don, telling him I wanted him to succeed in this venture but I didn't know what he was physically capable of doing. I said I did not want to give him tasks he could not do and I required his honesty if I asked him to do something he was not capable of doing or that would frustrate him. He seemed very appreciative of my directness and so things got off to a good start.

I had an empty desk on the side in my office where I set Don up to work. He had very limited use of his hands so he would position a metal rod with a hard rubber end in his mouth to turn the pages of our court documents. This method proved very effective back in the day when we would pick up stacks of computer printouts from the county IT department that had to be audited. For readers who recall these types of documents, I'm referring to those high stacks of connected green-and-white-lined computer paper with punch holes on both sides. Don could very easily use his mouth tool to flip these pages as he reviewed them for mistakes. His work was a huge help for the office and gave him an immediate sense of accomplishment, which is very important for anyone in an internship—physically challenged or not.

As Don shared my office, we often chatted and got to know each other. I discovered he grew up around Erie, Pennsylvania and was a die-hard fan of the Pittsburgh Steelers. I grew up on the other side of Pennsylvania and am an Eagles fan. (Had I known Don was a Steelers fan before hiring him, I may have made another choice! Just joking.) We had fun teasing each other about our favorite sports teams. I recall Don's face one Monday morning when he came into the office after the Eagles had beaten the Steelers the previous day. I had placed an Eagles poster above his desk—out of his reach! He protested in a teasing way about the unfairness of placing the poster where he could not take it down. We both enjoyed the joke, and it became part of our friendship. As with many things in life, there is great power in humor when used carefully.

I gained several valuable insights from having Don employed in our office. One was how his positive attitude brought out the best in those around him. People responded to him in an equally positive way and were willing to assist him whenever he needed help with a task. It warmed my heart every day to observe these interactions. Don would also share with me stories about how kind everyone was with him.

So what does "A Jerk of the Head Will Result in a Hat on the Sidewalk" have to do with Don? Actually, it's a quote from a story Don shared with me one day. He told me he had a hat he enjoyed wearing and, when he saw an attractive woman approaching, he would jerk his head a bit, and oops! His hat would fall off. The woman invariably would stop to assist him in putting his hat back on, which allowed him to strike up a conversation with her. What a sneaky guy! Of course he was single at the time, and now he has been happily married for several years. While writing this chapter, I learned from his wife she did not meet Don through this ruse of his. However, she did share other stories of him flirting with the young ladies while he was at ASU.

While Don's situation usually brought out the best in people, there were, unfortunately, a few times the worst side of human nature showed its ugly head as well. For example, he explained how he kept his money in a fanny pack on the back of his wheelchair. When he made a purchase, he would ask the vendor to retrieve his money and put the change back in the pack. A number of times, he told me, people would rip him off and he had no way of knowing this until he was back home and could review the amount of money in his wallet. Wow!

The main lesson I learned from hiring Don was not to allow my perception of someone's limitations stop me from letting them show me how they could shine. I must admit it took me another experience to have this lesson truly sink into my skull. Some 15 years after I hired Don, I was working at a different court in a different state when a deaf applicant applied for a position as a file clerk with us. My initial reaction, despite my experience with Don, was hesitation and reluctance. I caught myself wondering how she could function effectively with all the people with whom she would have to interact in her position.

Fortunately, others involved in the selection process prevailed and we agreed to interview her. We set up a laptop computer so we could type questions and answers back and forth. She nailed the interview and was hired. And, once again, my initial reservations proved to be completely unfounded as she turned out to be the best file clerk we ever employed. Like Don, her positive spirit inspired everyone. No one minded at all writing notes back and forth with her when needed. I guess the other real lesson I learned from both Don and from this woman is that I am a slow learner.

As we got to know each other better, Don revealed to me how he became a quadriplegic. When he was 17 years old he and some friends were at a favorite wimming hole outside of Pittsburgh. He was attempting a somersault from the bank. The bank was wet; his feet slipped and he broke his neck. He spent three years in a rehab facility. Don willingly shared his recovery challenges and the emotions he went through in coping with such a traumatic life-altering injury. He was candid about wishing he had died several times during his long recovery process. Through the help of many kind professionals, Don came to accept his limitations and decided to continue to live life to the fullest. I cannot begin to fathom what Don went through, but I am very glad he survived the accident as he is a positive force in a world that greatly needs people with his wonderful attitude.

Long story short, Don wound up getting a full-time job with the court and spent 26 years gainfully employed as a very productive member of the court family. He retired just a few years ago. I cannot begin to count the number of people I hired in my career, but I do know with certainty that hiring Don Thompson as an intern was one decision I will never regret. It had an amazing impact on his life, but more importantly it has influenced my thinking about the people I encounter in my life every day. Don is a good man who never saw his physical limitations as a disability—nor should anyone else. I am honored to call him a friend… even though he is a Steeler's fan.

RECIPE REMINDERS FOR A JERK OF THE HEAD WILL RESULT IN A HAT ON THE SIDEWALK

- Take a chance on people.
- Do not let your preconceived ideas about limits hold you or others back.
- Trust in your fellow humans that they are capable of their best!

11

Donald Thompson

STATEMENT FROM DON THOMPSON

I need to tip my hat to Lance for his candidness and friendship. He exposed me to the world of court administration. Prior to my accident, the only work experience I had was in construction and labor. The intricate workings of an office were a whole different world. Due to his ability to interact with judges, clerks and administrative personnel, I learned how to interact with so many colleagues.

Lance and I have remained close friends.

I owe thanks to my parents, siblings, extended family, friends, and the Lord for giving me the courage to start college, move to Arizona on my own and reach for my dreams.

Chapter 3

The Most Ignorant Man in The World

"He was a bold man that first ate an oyster."

–Jonathan Swift

Would you respect or even want to hang around someone whose stated goal was "to die the most ignorant man in the world"? Probably not, and neither would I. Or so I thought until I had the honor of knowing the person who said this, and his true intent behind this curious statement.

I am referring to the late Honorable Robert C. Broomfield, who started his judicial career in the Superior Court of Arizona for Maricopa County and whose last position was as a federal judge in the United States District Court for the District of Arizona. I am blessed to have had the opportunity to work with many intelligent, ethical, and highly motivated men and women. Judge Broomfield was one of them, but he impressed me in a different way, as he is one of the "curious" people I came across during my professional career—and one who deserves to be in anyone's cookbook of positive recipes for life.

Judge Broomfield was born on June 18, 1933 in Detroit, Michigan. He went to college at Pennsylvania State University where he earned his Bachelor of Science degree, followed by a law degree at the James E. Rogers College of Law at the University of Arizona. After eight years in private practice, he became a judge in the Superior Court of Arizona and served in that capacity until being appointed to the federal bench by President Ronald Reagan. Judge Broomfield passed away from cancer on July 10, 2014.

I first encountered Judge Broomfield when he was Presiding Judge in the Superior Court of Arizona in Maricopa County. This is the court of general jurisdiction located in Phoenix, Arizona. As Presiding Judge, Judge Broomfield was responsible for the administration of the court, with broad oversight for running the court but little formal authority to support the responsibility. A common joke about being a Presiding or Chief Judge in a court system is that it is like being a caretaker of a cemetery: you are over a lot of people, but no one is listening.

Despite little formal authority, when Judge Broomfield strode into a room it was obvious everyone respected his informal power. In the years I had the privilege of working with him, I never once saw him abuse this power or treat anyone with disrespect. He garnered the respect of his peers and subordinates by exhibiting the following traits: honesty, knowledge of the subject matter at hand, solid preparation, and a very important trait that is often left out of books on leadership: a continuously curious mind.

When Judge Broomfield announced to me that he hoped to die the most ignorant man in the world, I was dumbfounded as he was one of the most intelligent, thoughtful men I'd ever met. I couldn't understand why he would declare that he wished to be ignorant, but his meaning quickly became clear.

He explained that, as a trial judge, he was presented with new court cases every day, each with unfamiliar issues and new ideas. To prepare for each case he had to delve into (and fully comprehend) an entirely new set of facts about the situation at hand. His cases ranged from processes for manufacturing, new products being developed, unique contractual relationships, and other diverse subjects. All which required him to learn something new, which resulted in

14

Judge Broomfield realizing just how little he knew. The more he learned about the nuances of each case, the more he realized how much more there was to know. His statement about his desire to die "the most ignorant man alive" now made sense to me. It epitomized perfectly what it means to be a lifelong learner—a key trait for leaders and for anyone looking to live a fulfilling life.

Writing this chapter about dying as the most ignorant man in the world made me think about how we actually define ignorance. We usually think of it as someone who lacks knowledge and is not very smart. Of course, this is not at all what Judge Broomfield meant about himself. While I do not know all the reasons Judge Broomfield had such a stellar career as an attorney and a judge, I am sure his curiosity was a key reason behind his success. I saw him face many challenging situations in his role as Chief Judge, yet he treated each one with great interest. He asked critical questions to understand the issues and to figure out the intent of those involved. It was his deep sense of curiosity that made Judge Broomfield a great leader with a quiet, unassuming personality. Due to his passion for being a lifelong learner and his unquenchably curious mind, I am sure he passed away meeting his goal of dying the most ignorant man in the world.

Over the past several years I, too, have become a proponent of remaining curious and being a lifelong learner. Someone with a curious mind will seldom get bored. If you ever feel bored, walking through the doors of a public library can change that in a heartbeat. Just looking at the hundreds of shelves of books containing a wealth of information and stories about which you know very little should be enough to end your boredom. Realizing how much you can still learn about any topic is, to me, exhilarating. A consultant I worked with for years informed me that once a year he attends a conference completely out of his normal realm of consulting—a topic he knew nothing about. He did this to challenge himself to stay fresh, to remain curious, and to be a lifelong learner.

Thinking about curious minds reminds me of the powerful book, *The Marriages Between Zones Two, Three, and Four* by the Nobel Prize-winning author, Doris Lessing, which I shall quickly summarize. In this book, Lessing creates a world in which people live in five different zones with distinct boundaries that they sometimes cross on horseback. The people in Zone Four invest all their time, money, and energy into protecting their borders, despite the fact there was never a known attack from either neighboring zone. In contrast, the people in Zone Three are pacifists who spend all their time focusing on the arts and other creative endeavors. One day, a resident of Zone Four explains to a person from Zone Three that his zone has a law that prevents their citizens from gazing up at the blue, misty mountain ranges of Zone Three. If someone is caught looking up at Zone Three, their punishment is to wear a very heavy helmet on their head to prevent them from looking up. The resident of Zone Three is appalled, as she feels it is barbaric to punish someone for looking beyond their current boundaries. In essence, Zone Four residents are being punished for being curious, looking at new ideas, and finding new ways of thinking and of living.

But something even more troubling dawns on the Zone Three resident. She realizes that inhabitants of her zone never look at the peaceful mountains of Zone Two because they are complacent. Unlike the residents of Zone Four, who have a law prohibiting people from looking to Zone Three, her people are permitted to do so, but they never do. They are so content that they have lost their curiosity.

Lessing's message is clear: we often put limitations on our thinking and our willingness to move beyond our current boundaries, not because anyone is prohibiting us from doing so, but simply because we become complacent like the people living in Zone Three. A blessing we all share is that no one forbids you from looking at distant horizons. No one is forcing you to wear a helmet to keep your head down. There is no law preventing you from being inquisitive. It is up to you to never be complacent about your own learning. I implore you to take on Judge Broomfield's approach to life and to strive every day to become a life-long learner.

RECIPE REMINDERS FOR THE MOST IGNORANT MAN IN THE WORLD

- Good leaders possess two important traits: humility and curiosity.
- When presented with a difficult challenge or new situation, stay curious.
- A curious mind never gets bored.

P.S. Here is one last intriguing story about my friendship with Judge Broomfield. I grew up in the beautiful farmlands of Lancaster County, Pennsylvania, outside the small borough of Marietta. When I first met Judge Broomfield, he mentioned that his mother's family was from the same area. He did not know much about his mother's side of the family. Several years later, he came into my office to tell me about a recent visit he made to Lancaster County in search of relatives. He said he had little success. I asked him his mother's maiden name. "Hiestand," he said, to which I responded that my parents had actually purchased the old Heistand mansion and that I was born and raised in that house. We were both astounded at this coincidence, having known each other for many years before recognizing that we shared such a meaningful connection. Small world!

Chapter 4

Lessons from A Broken Plate

"My recipe for dealing with anger and frustration: set the kitchen timer for twenty minutes, cry, rant and rave, and at the sound of the bell, simmer down and go about business as usual."

–Phyllis Diller

What can we learn about the power of forgiveness from a broken plate at a potluck party? How about lessons like the harm we do to ourselves by not forgiving others, like letting go of resentments, and not being so hard on others since we have no idea what they may be going through? How about learning to get off of our self-righteous soapboxes for a few minutes?

I learned many of these lessons by the simple act of breaking a plate at an office potluck party many, many years ago. It's interesting I do not remember the exact year, nor who was at the event, nor even the reason it was being held, but I do recall it as if was yesterday—dropping the plate and the consequences my accident set off.

My lack of a clear memory about other details of this day is understandable since I have heard the brain encodes traumatic memories but lets go of insignificant events that happened around the same time. For example, depending on your age, if I ask where you were when President Kennedy was shot, or when John Lennon was shot, or when you first heard of the planes crashing into the World Trade Towers, you will likely have strong recall of where you were and what you were doing at the time. If I asked what you were doing the day before these events, or just other details of the same day, those memories are likely long gone for you.

Returning to my accident, I recall having played some role in organizing the potluck as it was for someone in our office who was leaving or celebrating some achievement. I also recall being somewhat surprised when a woman in our office strode in with her boyfriend who worked for a different agency. We usually did not encourage outside participation in our events, but this celebration was not such a big deal. And since he appealed to our better angels by bringing a plate of cookies, so no one asked him to leave. Little did I know, at the time, how this man's showing up at this event would linger in my memory for decades—and, unfortunately, not in a good way.

As the luncheon died down, I wound up being one of just a few people who lingered to clean up. I was a bit frustrated at the lack of help, so my level of resentment was already a bit high. To make things worse, as I took the plate that the boyfriend of the coworker had brought to the sink to rinse it off, it suddenly slipped from my hands and shattered into a million pieces on the linoleum floor.

When I was done cleaning up, I walked to the office of the owner of the now shattered plate, to inform him what happened. I immediately apologized for the mishap. In my mind it was just a glass plate, so I did not expect the reaction I received. Upon telling him I accidently broke the plate, he totally lost it. He flipped out and went off on me. He stated that the plate he'd brought was a family heirloom from his great-grandmother and that it was "priceless."

I do not recall exactly how the conversation that day ended, other than there was no softening on his part about how upset he was about this. And since this was a so-called priceless family heirloom, there was nothing I could do to replace this lost relic. But I recall my thought process going something like this: First, why in the world would you have brought something so valuable to a potluck? Second, why didn't you take it with you at the end of the party, if it was truly an irreplaceable family heirloom? And, last but not least, why didn't you stay and help clean up?! I possibly even went on to think, "Why were you even there in the first place, you jerk?"

Today I wonder what was going on in his world that day to make him react that way. I have no idea, but now with more life experiences under my belt, I try to be more empathetic when stuff like this happens. I remind myself I have never walked in that person's shoes and I do not know what stresses they might be under. I focus on what I do not know about that person in that moment and I try not to take events like this personally. But, way back then, I just got all furious and self-righteous—a total waste of time and energy.

When it comes to forgiveness and what we do to ourselves when we do not forgive, I have to admit I held onto my anger at him for many, many years! Every time I would think of this incident and his blasting me for an innocent mistake, I could feel my arteries closing up. I am pretty sure the guy whose plate I broke forgot about it soon after it happened, but I was not so lucky. It stuck in my craw for far too long—and to what end? What good did it do for me to stay angry about this silly incident? None.

Now when some incident happens and I feel my temperature rising, I try to remember to get *curious, not furious.* As I believe we learn best when we have to teach about a topic, I developed a program along these lines titled "Get Curious, Not Furious." In my talk, after reviewing the negative health effects of closing up our arteries about something over which we have no control, I share several techniques to cope with anger-inducing situations in a healthier way. Some of these involve mindfulness activities, such as deep breathing, visualizing having a different reaction, or asking yourself why you were upset on this exact same day one year ago. I like this last question, as it serves to remind us that most of the things we get upset about will pass and we do not even recall them a year later. The challenge is to move past our anger and frustration quickly and in a healthy way.

There are endless examples of people and communities who faced senseless, unthinkable acts of violence perpetrated upon them, and who seek to find ways to forgive the person or people who caused them harm rather than wishing them ill. A couple notable examples come to mind. One of these examples is how the congregants of the Emanuel African Methodist Episcopal Church in downtown Charleston, South Carolina responded after Dylann Roof murdered nine of their congregants while they sat in prayer in the basement of the church. Roof's stated motive for the shooting was to invoke a race riot. But rather than giving him this satisfaction, most of the congregants of this church did just the opposite—they forgave him. Their expression of love and compassion as they faced immeasurable tragedy and grief demonstrates a strength of willpower that I am not sure I could muster if faced with a similar situation.

Another noteworthy example is how Nelson Mandela responded to a question from former President Bill Clinton about his feelings toward those who held him captive in a cell in South Africa for 27 years. As reported in an article by Justice Malala that appeared in *The Telegraph* on December 7, 2013

Bill Clinton, the former US president, told the United Nations in July 2013 how he [Clinton] had raised with Mandela his decision to invite his jailer to his inauguration and bring white opposition parties into his government. Mr. Clinton asked Mandela: "Tell me the truth: when you were walking down the road that last time, didn't you hate them?" Mandela answered: "I did. I am old enough to tell the truth [...] I felt hatred and fear but I said to myself, if you hate them when you get in that car you will still be their prisoner. I wanted to be free and so I let it go."

Just as Nelson Mandela did not permit his jailers to have control over his emotions after he was released, and the survivors of the Charleston church shooting did not permit Dylann Roof to have control over them after the shooting, I wish I had their strength of character after something as insignificant and silly as being yelled at over an accidentally broken plate!

The key to unlocking the gift of forgiveness that works for me, most of the time, is, again, to have curiosity about the other party. This curiosity has two distinct levels. First, remain curious about why the event happened or why the person or group of people did what you find offensive or wrong. Second, and more important in my estimation, is to remain curious about why *you* are offended or upset about the situation. What is going on inside you to cause your reaction? What from your childhood or past triggers something in your brain that causes you to be upset?

I have witnessed many situations where two people experience the exact same event, yet one is highly offended while the other is not. Pondering on this, one can make the argument there is no objective reality that triggers the reaction. Rather, it is one person's previous experiences or their sense of right and wrong that cause them to react in a certain way. The challenge we all face is to react with love and compassion rather than with hatred and fury.

I opened this chapter with a quote from Phyllis Diller: "My recipe for dealing with anger and frustration: set the kitchen timer for twenty minutes, cry, rant and rave, and at the sound of the bell, simmer down and go about business as usual." I think this is sound advice, as it is certainly acceptable to "cry, rant and rave" when we are upset about something. We need to get these

23

feelings out or risk internal damage to our heart and arteries. But, as Ms. Diller famously suggests, we then need to move on and get back to business as usual. And, finally, remember, when selecting a plate to take to a potluck, please leave the priceless family heirlooms in the china cabinet!

RECIPE REMINDERS FROM LESSONS FROM
A BROKEN PLATE

- Be cautious when feeling a noble sense of right and wrong, as it can get you into trouble—physically and emotionally. This is not to say you should not stand up in the face of grave injustice, but think about whether you are overreacting to a minor infringement.

- We need to forgive others as much for ourselves as for their sake, as we are often just punishing ourselves more by holding onto our anger.

- Forgiveness is an amazing antidote to hate and violence.

Chapter 5

An Inspirational Oil Change

"My recipe for life is not being afraid of myself, afraid of what I think or of my opinions."

–Eartha Kitt

Have you ever taken on a project or task and dreaded it, only to discover it proved to be inspirational? I had just that experience recently when I drove my car into the shop for a long overdue oil change. Now, you wouldn't think an oil change could turn out to be an exciting journey, but here's what happened.

With umpteen places from which to choose, I resorted to the easiest: the car dealer where I bought my car. I wanted to get this task crossed off my to-do list on my way to work, but I dreaded how much time the appointment would take. So, in an attempt to beat the crowd, I pulled into the staging area at the car dealer about 20 minutes before they opened. As I rounded the corner, whoa! To my shock, there were already at least ten other people who had the same idea and were already ahead of me in line. I quickly realized it was not going to be the speedy oil change I had hoped for, and I began dreading the wait.

Once the dealer opened I checked in and was informed it would take three hours for them just to get started on my car. Rather than wait in their lounge and be tempted by the stale donuts, I put my name on the list for the free shuttle they offered so I could get a ride to my office. By now I was falling into "worst-case scenario" thinking, as I envisioned the driver of the courtesy van needing to drop off at least a dozen other people before reaching my building as his last stop. My mind raced with negative emotions, wishing I had never decided to do this darn oil change.

To my shock the van driver, a man in his early 60's, came into the waiting room within minutes and called my name—and my name only! Sweet. I would be alone in the van and, thus, would have a direct ride to downtown.

I got into the white courtesy van and we departed. Despite my introvert instinct to start checking e-mails or looking at my phone, pretending to be busy to avoid having to make small talk with this total stranger, I stepped outside of my comfort zone and started a discussion with him. This is when my day made a complete 180-degree turn and taught me yet another lesson in positive thinking.

I asked the van driver about his job and if he enjoyed it. In reply, he shared an amazing and inspirational story with me. He related how he had retired about two years ago from driving a beverage delivery truck, which he had done for the same company for about 30 years. He told me he loved that job, but his body could no longer tolerate loading and unloading cases of soft drinks all day long. After retiring, he spent about a year tackling projects around his house he never had time to finish while working full-time. After these home improvements were finished he got bored, as he was used to being super busy. So he announced to his spouse he was going to find someone to pay him to have fun. She laughed at his statement and said, "Good luck with that goal!"

The van driver—let's call him Alex, as I do not recall his name—began a search process by first listing his likes and dislikes about his previous job. Through this analysis he realized that he really loved driving and having interactions with different people as he made deliveries. He also realized that the only thing he didn't like about his previous job, and the primary reason he retired, was the heavy lifting involved.

This thinking helped him narrow down his job search and bingo! When he saw the dealership job ad seeking a courtesy van driver, he knew it was for him. He applied and a few weeks later they called him in for a job interview. He so impressed them during this meeting that they actually offered him a car sales job that would have garnered a much larger salary than a courtesy van driver. They were amazed when he turned them down, insisting that he only wanted the courtesy van driver position. To his surprise, they informed him that job was no longer available and they graciously parted ways.

Alex continued to check back with the auto company every few weeks, reminding them he was still interested in the courtesy van driver position should it become available. Then, a few months later, his phone rang and he heard the voice of his contact from the auto company on the other end. He was thrilled they called to offer him the job as the van driver.

At the time I had my chance encounter with him, he had had the job for about a year. He related to me how much he loved the interaction with the customers like me, and being able to do something he loved—drive—without having to load and unload any merchandise. He laughed as we both agreed that he had literally found a company to pay him to have fun.

As I think back on Alex, I garnered three key takeaways from him. First, we need to constantly remind ourselves to be open to new experiences and not to expect the worst. In my case, I dreaded the perceived waste of time, not the oil change. But it turned into a good learning experience for me, listening to

Alex's story. Second, if you are introverted like me, it's not hard to break out of your instincts and take a chance on engaging in discussion with, yes, a stranger. Every discussion can, and usually does, have some sort of lesson to teach you. With Alex, I walked away with a warm feeling, realizing there is great value in sharing our life stories with others. And, third, let's remember life should be fun! Even a job can be fun. If your work isn't fun right now, try doing what Alex did: make a list of what you enjoy and do not enjoy about your work, and then go out and find a company that will pay you to have fun.

RECIPE REMINDERS FOR AN INSPIRATIONAL OIL CHANGE

- Go into every experience expecting the unexpected to turn out great—and you will most likely be pleasantly rewarded. Positive events start with positive thinking.

- Do not be shy about interacting with strangers. If you are introverted, focus not on your fear of talking to others, but on what you might learn from them.

Chapter 6

For the Love of Angela

"Cooking is like love. It should be entered into
with abandon or not at all."
–Harriet van Horne

What is the hardest thing you have done in your life? For some, sporting accomplishments such as completing an Ironman Triathlon or their first running marathon may come to mind. For others, the answer could be obtaining some degree or starting a new job. Yes, these are worthy achievements, and ones that are deserving of celebration. For others, saying goodbye to a loved one or telling a child about the death of a parent or grandparent might come to mind. Or how about carrying a pregnancy to birth if you knew there was no chance the newborn child would survive outside the womb? This recipe of dishing up food for thought is about one person, one very exceptional person, who said "Yes" to this heart-wrenching question.

Prior to continuing, I recognize that for some the questions posed above may touch on the very sensitive topic of abortion. My intent in sharing this story is to speak to the challenges in facing any difficult decision, and to stress it is how we deal with tragedy—and what we do after the fact—that shows our true character. My purpose is not to enter into a debate on the abortion question or to touch those understandably sensitive issues; it is just that there is no way to tell this story without raising the questions posed above.

This individual I am referring to, who I am honored to call a friend, is Ms. Nancy Mayer-Whittington. Nancy had a long, stellar career as the Clerk of Court for the United States District Court for the District of Columbia. While her work had a lasting impact on many people, equally important is the positive impact she continues to have on so many people since she retired. Nancy continues inspiring others year after year, yet with great modesty and reserve.

I shared Nancy's story in a speech at a national conference a few years back. We were at a gathering of the Clerks of Court for the United States District Courts throughout the country, of which both Nancy and I were members. There are 94 different districts, and each has a Clerk of Court who serves as its chief administrative officer. Although this group of executives meets formally only every other year, this is a close-knit group. Most know each other on a professional and personal level. This was not a group of strangers to Nancy, thus I felt comfortable sharing her very personal story with those in attendance. Nancy had no idea I was going to give these remarks. Here is what I shared about Nancy at this conference, with only slight changes in the wording:

The eighth habit of highly successful people in Dr. Stephen Covey's book, *The 8th Habit*, is to "Find your voice and inspire others to find theirs." I stand before you today to recognize our peer, Nancy Mayer-Whittington, as an outstanding example of someone who, through terrible adversity, found her voice and inspired others to find theirs.

I do so as we need to celebrate and share each other's accomplishments. I know Nancy is too humble to share the achievement of which I am about to speak, but I believe it needs to be shared as it is a truly moving story. Telling it may be hard for me to get through, so please bear with me.

Do you remember where you were or what you were doing on November 17, 1994? Probably not. I know I do not. Nancy does, as she was in a delivery room giving birth to Angela, her beautiful daughter. However, she was giving birth under the saddest of circumstances, after having been informed in her first trimester of pregnancy that her baby had Trisomy 18—a condition that, according to the doctor, was "incompatible with life." On November 17, 1994, a day I assume when most of us have no memory of where we were or what we were doing, our peer and friend, Nancy, was giving birth to a daughter she knew would not live long after birth, if she were even born alive. Had she lived, Angela would have turned 14 last month.

While few of us have gone through this type of unthinkable heart-wrenching experience, it is how we deal with tragedy that shines a light on one's true character. In 2007, Nancy published this book: *For the Love of Angela.*

In it, she brought her voice and Angela's to the world. As Stephen Covey says of our voice: "It is the voice of the human spirit—full of hope and intelligence, resilient by nature, boundless in its potential to serve the common good." Covey goes on to say our "voice is of unique personal significance—

significance that is revealed as we face out greatest challenges and which makes us equal to them."

I cannot say this nearly as eloquently as did Nancy in her book, so here is the opening paragraph from her introduction:

I began this book to stop myself from drowning. I thought that writing down my experiences would reveal the true meaning of my daughter Angela's brief life, and I could finally come up for air. As with most things in life, however, what one has in mind at the beginning is not always what happens in the end.... Sometimes the meaning of tragic events is revealed and we fail to recognize it. We are often too angry to do so at first, or we refuse to believe that any good can come from a tragic situation. To be honest, there is nothing good about the death of a child. It is the life you lead afterwards that creates good. It is the integration of that child's heart and soul into your being that transforms you and makes you the person you become. You can ignore this evolution, reject it, or be oblivious to it. The alternative is to accept it, reflect on it, and grow beautiful because of it. The choice is yours.

In addition to writing *For the Love of Angela*, Nancy is the co-founder of Isaiah's Promise, a support group for parents continuing a pregnancy after a severe or fatal diagnosis. In that role, Nancy has helped numerous parents through extremely difficult times. She shared a story with me about how she was actually in the delivery room with a family and it was anticipated the baby would not be born alive. Nancy recounted: "The baby was born alive, opened his eyes, and looked around before he passed away. It was a miracle." The baby exceeded all medical expectations and experienced seeing his mother's face prior to passing away.

Nancy referencing this as a "miracle" demonstrates the choices we all have, regardless of the situation we face. It is a choice to look for something positive, a choice to look beyond our limited understanding of a situation, and a choice to make our voice known, in a positive, uplifting way, in the face of our greatest challenges like Nancy did in writing *For the Love of Angela* and in forming Isaiah's Promise.

Thank you, Nancy. Thank you for your resilience. Thank you for making the world a better place. Thank you for founding Isaiah's Promise through which you have helped numerous families. Thank you for sharing Angela with the world. Thank you for finding and sharing your voice.

That concluded my remarks to the group, but the experience was powerful and has remained with me all these years. I recall how there were very few dry eyes in the packed conference room as I concluded my talk, myself included. And therein is part of the moral.

In thinking about this event, I have come to see that just as we need to find more ways to celebrate together, equally important is to be human enough to share all our emotions with others. This includes our tears and our grief, as these are the signs of being truly human and being in touch with our collective humanity. Heck, I still cry just thinking about Lassie being missing. (For any Millennials reading this, Google "Lassie" and you'll know what I mean.)

A side effect of my speech that I did not anticipate was how heartwarming it felt to see everyone embracing Nancy at the end of the day. Several people approached me, as well, and thanked me for sharing the story and for letting my own emotions out, as I sniffled and choked on tears a few times during the speech.

Nancy's book is still available, and I encourage everyone to read it. It is moving, thoughtful, and enlightening, raising issues most of us have likely never pondered. For example, Nancy cites how the doctors informed her that her baby's condition would be "incompatible with life." I do not fault the doctors for using this term; sometimes there is simply no good way to convey a tragic message. But reading that phrase in her book made me realize how our self-imposed definitions often limit our understanding and thinking about something. I know the doctors were meaning to gently suggest that Angela would not live long, if at all, after birth. But, on the other hand, Angela's short time on earth was not actually incompatible with life if we consider what she brought to the world. Of course, we all would have wanted Angela to live a long and healthy life, just as with any child, but a very brief life does not make it "incompatible with life," does it?

In her book, Nancy also writes about the internal struggle she faced when determining how to respond and how much information to share with well-meaning people who approached her during her pregnancy and offered congratulations or asked questions about the baby. For strangers, it seemed obvious she need not share that Angela had Trisomy 18. But with close friends, how to respond was not so clear. For most friends, she would usually inform them of the situation and that Angela would not live outside the womb. Understandably, this left most people speechless. As Nancy wrote in her book, "They had no idea what to say and just nodded wordlessly as I tried to comfort them." The irony of the situation was darkly profound. Suddenly, the person who needed comforting the most wound up comforting others. This took a great deal of strength on Nancy's part, but I am equally confident it aided to her healing process as well.

One of Nancy's many touching experiences shared in her book is how giving birth to Angela changed her perspective on fear. Prior to Angela, much of Nancy's motivation was fear-based: "the fear of failure, the fear of disappointing someone, the fear of being alone, the fear of not living up to my potential, and my biggest fear, that of losing a child." Angela changed all of this for Nancy; she was no longer driven by fear but, as she wrote, by "the love of one four-pound, eight-ounce masterpiece."

We all should look deeply at our fears and find a recipe for motivation and determination based on something more positive, more resilient, and more powerful than the fear itself. Perhaps that something is love! Actually, I believe a loving attitude with a huge dose of forgiveness for those we deem to have wronged us can overcome any fear.

What are my main takeaways from giving this speech, and from having the honor of knowing Nancy? One is we need to share our personal stories more, as doing so gives others a chance to do the same and makes us more human. I also learned to not get too hung up on the outcome I expect from a situation, and to find ways to make the best of whatever happens.

I can think of no better way to close this chapter than with the closing Nancy used in her book. "Life, then, is a journey from birth to death, with the goal of leaving the world a slightly better place. As Mother Teresa said, 'We can do no great things, only small things with great love.' Small things, done in Angela's name, with great love, have been and are my legacy. And so, the journey continues."

RECIPE REMINDERS FOR *"FOR THE LOVE OF ANGELA"*

- Freedom of choice: We have a choice in how we respond to any situation. This does not mean we should not grieve or cry; that is part of being human and of healing. What it does mean, though, is we can choose to have a positive view of any event, and that will be our legacy of it. If you doubt this, I encourage you to read Victor Frankl's *Man's Search for Meaning* about his experience in a Nazi concentration camp.

- Find a way to bring your voice to the world: We all have a positive story to tell, a way to improve at least one person's day, something to share to make the world a better place. Please find a way to bring your voice out in a positive way.

- Stay true to your values and convictions: Nancy did this by bringing Angela into the world, and we are all better off for her doing so. If you would like to read Nancy's book, visit her website www.fortheloveofangela.com where you can purchase a copy.

STATEMENT FROM NANCY MEYER WHITTINGTON

Miracles come in all shapes and sizes. The miracle you receive may not be the one for which you prayed. However, that miracle just might be the best thing that has ever happened to you.

Angela is my miracle. I am blessed to witness all the joy she has inspired.

Through Angela's legacy, Isaiah's Promise, we strive to help families re-frame their expectations of having the perfect child and to accept the child they are going to have. We ask them to embrace Robert Frost's words when he describes one consequence of choice, "Two paths diverged in the wood, and I – I took the one less traveled by, and that has made all the difference."

Chapter 7

All It Takes Is One—What's Your Cause?

"It was improv that really helped me start coming up with recipes and just believe in my instincts. That's why the first recipe I made up was 'I Ain't Chicken Chicken' because I finally felt bold and fearless in the kitchen, which was an entirely new feeling for me."

–Aarti Sequeira

"All it takes is one. What's your cause?" the young man shouted over and over again to the squirming crowd as we waited for Old Faithful to erupt in Yellowstone National Park. I can still hear his voice, despite the years that have passed, as his statement had a powerful impact on me.

We were on vacation in this amazing park for a few days. Most of our days had been spent in the less remote areas like the Lamar Valley region where we had spotted bears, wolves, and other wildlife. Of course, we planned to do the more touristy stuff, like visiting Old Faithful, along with hundreds of other visitors who likewise had scribed this natural wonder on their vacation to-do list.

It was a burning hot, humid day in mid-August, and we were waiting for the show. But Old Faithful was being somewhat stubborn in her normal predictability. The time posted on the sign indicating when she was going to erupt had come and gone. People were getting restless.

If you've never been to see Old Faithful, let me set the stage. The geyser sits in a large lava field, surrounded by a semi-circle of stands strategically placed about fifty yards back from where she spouts her infamous fountain of steam. The seating is similar to the common metal bleachers at your local little league baseball park, with six rows of seats on each stand ascending steeply upwards. Their most distinguishing characteristic, of course, is how uncomfortable and hard they are to sit on.

A few feet in front of the bleachers is a small, solid barricade in a ring, only about eighteen inches high. The inside wall of this barricade is dotted with signs warning spectators to stay behind for their own safety and to protect the environment around Old Faithful.

The seating area held, I would guess, 300 to 400 people. Being the middle of August, peak tourist season, the stands were packed with travelers from all over the world. The site is totally exposed, with no relief from the blazing sun. So we waited, sweating profusely, cameras in hand, anxious for Old Faithful to surprise and thrill us.

As she fell further and further behind her scheduled eruption time, the crowd grew more and more restless. Almost everyone was squirming around, trying to find a comfortable way to sit on the benches that were as hard as the dried lava that surrounded us. People could be heard complaining about the delay, as if nature was at their beck and call. They kept glancing anxiously at their watches, some groaning aloud about their self-imposed time schedule. As the minutes crawled by, some families actually got up and left, apparently deciding the wait was not worth it. Impatience was taking over, and I found myself slipping into the same state of mind.

All of a sudden, to our surprise, a young man in his early 20s—a clean-cut blond who looked like a college cheerleader or gymnast—stepped over the small barricade in front of the seating area. My first thought, being the rule-follower I am, was something like, "Hey, you can't do that. Don't you see the signs warning you to stay back? What do you think you are doing?" Fortunately, I kept my thoughts to myself for a change, and sat back to see what he was going to do.

Standing in the restricted zone, the rabble-rouser began trying to persuade the crowd to join him in doing the wave—you know, the activity you see at football games and other sporting events where a section of spectators in the bleachers stand up, throw their arms in the air, sit down, and then the sections next to them do the same thing, consecutively in rapid progression. Eventually, it looks like an ocean wave moving through the stadium as people stand up and down, throwing their arms into the air, section by section.

"Ah, a troublemaker," I thought to myself. But he persisted, slowly and deliberately moving back and forth in front of each section of bleachers at a time, six feet in one direction and then back to where he started, over and over again. He acted so enthusiastically that the wave started to catch on. After he got one section excited, he moved down the line to the next, but just far enough so he could quickly jump back to the first section so they wouldn't lose their enthusiasm. He paraded from one section to another, eventually covering the entire group of stands, throwing his arms in the air with such passion and wild abandon that it was almost impossible not to participate in this spontaneous experience.

Except for me. I was still working at getting over my discomfort with his being on the wrong side of the barricade. My brain kept screaming, "You're in the DANGER zone, don't you see that?" I sat there stone still, adamantly refusing to warm up to the experience and let go of my inhibitions. I was actually never one to go in for that type of activity at sporting events anyway, so I just crossed my arms in defiance, even as others around me started doing the wave.

Eventually, though I don't know how or why, his passion and excitement won me over. I was feeling like an old stuck-in-the-mud die-hard, but I soon found myself standing and cheering wildly with the rest of the folks in my section as he ran past. I finally let go, and got totally silly, something I had almost never done. It was a unique and joyful feeling for me, and I honestly began to enjoy it.

The enthusiast kept moving around the semi-circle of bleachers until the entire crowd was participating in his spontaneous wave after wave. He ran back and forth several times to keep the movement going, faster and faster. When he finished and walked past the now laughing crowd, he put one arm high in the air, held up his finger and yelled, "All it takes is one. What's your cause?" He said this repeatedly as he walked past the various sections of bleachers. Then, just as he had appeared out of nowhere, he disappeared back into the crowd.

I recall my reaction to this astonishing performance very clearly. Here was this person—just another tourist on vacation—who took it upon himself, in a matter of about 90 seconds, to transform a frustrated, impatient crowd of complete strangers into a unified group of laughing, happy people. That sticky summer morning in Yellowstone National Park, he had a cause, executed it flawlessly, and proved that "all it takes is one."

This wave experience rooted in my mind because it taught me three lessons. First, after coming home, I began reflecting on why this crowd, myself included, was getting so antsy waiting for Old Faithful to erupt. My conclusion was that the signs around Old Faithful listed specific times she was supposed to perform her magic, and, when this marvel of nature failed to abide by the posted sign, we humans became restless because our expectation was not being net. Even sitting in the pristine, natural beauty of Yellowstone, we could not let go of our expectations for life to behave as we wanted it to. I wondered, what if the sign had read something like this instead: "Old Faithful will likely, but not necessarily, go off sometime between 10:00 a.m. and 10:30 a.m. this morning. Until she does so, relax and enjoy the scenery and each other."

Would this gentle and amusing language have improved the situation? Would it have changed the crowd's attitude? Possibly. But I am not sure, because the second lesson I learned is that even on vacation people seem to have a hard time abandoning their need for schedules and "accomplishing" stuff. Even in the unstructured landscape of nature, people want precision and structure. Like many spectators around me, I had a mental list of what I wanted to accomplish that day, and Mother Nature was not cooperating with *my* to-do list. How dare she do that to me! Shouldn't being on vacation be a time to stop worrying about our schedules and time frames?

Perhaps the most important lesson I learned that day, however, is that we all have the ability to make someone's day, to make others laugh, and to change a situation from negative to positive. Whether it's directed at one person or a crowd, the enthusiasm, passion, and commitment of a single person can inspire others to look at a situation differently and even to enjoy life in a childlike way again.

It reminds me of one of the few TV commercials I have ever appreciated: the Liberty Mutual Insurance "Pay It Forward" advertisement, where one person does something nice—an act of kindness—for a stranger. That kindness is then observed by someone else, who then does something nice for another stranger. In the commercial, a series of continuous, passed-on, random acts of kindness goes on until the act of kindness comes full circle to the first person who initiated the chain.

It's not that we all should perform acts of kindness or take risks to get something in return (although I think it usually does). The point is simply that we all have the opportunity to help others by performing a beneficial action. In effect, it is our own voluntary good deeds that contribute to making the world a better place. We cook up the positive when we make a difference in people's lives and in the world by our actions, especially when we use our talents to make other people smile.

Many people simply do not take these steps and I acknowledge, with regret, that there have been numerous times when I, too, missed such opportunities. I believe a key reason that we do not take these opportunities is our fear of failure. Many of us fear taking risks out of a concern that they may not pay off or that the risk may make us feel foolish if it does not turn out the way we hope. But this means that we are thinking about ourselves, rather than others.

I now have a plaque on my desk that reads: "What would you do if you knew you could not fail?" I look at it often as it reminds me to take more risks. Interestingly, I once shared it with a good friend, a professional artist, and his equally profound response was: "Why would I do anything if there was no chance of failure?" Wow! What a fresh and different perspective on this quote. Maybe I need a second plaque?

These two quotes make me think: what if no one had accepted the young man's lead and jumped into doing the wave with him? What would he have lost? What was the true risk he was taking? Would he have been embarrassed? Shamed? Disappointed? Maybe, but what was the risk of not trying? Not trying would have been accepting the crowd becoming more and more restless and unhappy. This young man took a risk and succeeded, and I have a feeling he felt confident in doing it as he knew his enthusiasm would carry the day.

I cited Aarti Sequeira at the beginning of this essay: "It was improv that really helped me start coming up with recipes and just believe in my instincts.

finally felt bold and fearless in the kitchen, which was an entirely new feeling for me." Climbing over a barrier and succeeding in getting a large group of strangers to do something as silly as a wave is a fantastic example of improv at its finest. And Sequeira's reference to feeling bold and fearless resonates with me as I, too, was stepping out of my-comfort zone to do something I had never done before.

So whether you are in the kitchen or out in nature waiting for a geyser to erupt, remember: we dish up food for thought in a positive way when we do improv in life, when we take risks to help others, when we shout to the world: "All it takes is one. What's your cause?"

RECIPE REMINDERS FOR ALL IT TAKES IS ONE—WHAT'S YOUR CAUSE?

- Figure out what your cause is and take risks to make it happen. This young man's cause that morning in Yellowstone National Park was to change the attitude of a restless crowd, which he did very effectively. Make a list of your causes and make a plan to bring them to fruition.

- Be willing to surprise yourself by stepping outside the box (or over the rail, in this case). This is a message for anyone—a reminder to not be so stuffy, to not be afraid to look silly, to stay curious to all experiences, to do the wave!

- Be flexible. Even if you have a to-do list for the day, build in the unexpected as the unexpected is sure to come your way. Just because you do not complete your list, the day can still be a grand success.

- Pay attention to those already engaged and on board with your cause. The young man creating the wave paid as much attention to those he already had fully engaged with him as he did with those he was still trying to get committed. This is an important message for all leaders, as all too often too much energy is spent on those not engaged when some part of the focus still needs to be on those fully on board with you.

Chapter 8

Kip the Moving Guy

"Recipes are important but only to a point. What's more important than recipes is how we think about food, and a good cookbook should open up a new way of doing just that."

–Michael Symon

With the exception of four to five hours sleep on Saturday night, we had all worked virtually 72 hours straight since Friday. With one notable exception, by Sunday night all of us were exhausted and grumpy. This one exception is a person I know only as "Kip the Moving Guy," and I learned a powerful lesson from him. This story illustrates how our internal language impacts our attitude and outlook. It is a testament to the power of a one-letter word – "I" – and its derivatives like "me" and "my." Kip the Moving Guy cooked up a positive experience for me during an enormously stressful weekend. I do not know Kip's full name so, Mr. Mystery Man, if you are out there somewhere reading this, please get in touch with me so I can give you proper credit in the next printing of this book.

The story unfolds as my colleagues and I were preparing to move from an old courthouse to a new one. Having the court shut down for even a day was not an option, so this relocation required moving eight judges' chambers and courtroom supplies, over 120 employees' offices, and all the related computers and equipment over one weekend. All operations went dark on a Friday at 5:00 p.m. and the court had to be up and operational by Monday morning at 8:00 a.m., as one of the judges had scheduled a jury trial for that morning.

While several court employees would be present all weekend to oversee the move, a private moving company had been hired to do the actual work. Kip was one of their employees. As this was a huge move over a very short period of time, the moving company also hired about 15 day workers to assist with the heavy lifting. We started on Friday night at 5:00 p.m. and lugged out desks, furniture, boxes, and computers until about midnight. We stopped for the night, agreeing to be back at 6:00 a.m. sharp the next morning. We were back at it Saturday morning before dawn. We were all a bit weary from lack of sleep, but massive amounts of hot coffee and sugar-laced donuts kept us hauling through the morning. As the day proceeded, it became apparent to everyone that one of the moving company employees—this fellow, Kip—was hustling much faster and was much more upbeat than any of the others. It wasn't that the other workers had a problem; it was simply that Kip's enthusiasm and positive attitude were patently obvious to all. He had an energy aura that glowed and radiated out to anyone working around him.

Kip's energy was so strong that as different crews were formed to tackle a specific office or an entire floor, the court staff all maneuvered to attempt to get Kip on their team. They would each claim to need Kip's help, even if it wasn't clear why.

Kip's energy never diminished on Saturday. As 6:00 p.m. approached and those in charge realized we would have to work very late into the night to accomplish what had to be moved that day, all the temporary workers said they had had enough and literally walked off the job. They hadn't expected to work

Saturday night, and they refused the extra time.

I will refrain from citing the language that the moving company employees screamed at the fleeing day laborers, imploring them to stay on the job site. Their attempts failed, and we wound up with just eight moving company staff and an equal number of court personnel remaining to continue working late into the night. We were 16 people doing the job of 30.

Since Kip was an employee of the moving company, he was one who remained. And his positive attitude and high spirits never wavered. Our reduced crew worked until 1:00 a.m. the following morning and finally called it quits, once again agreeing to be back at 6:00 a.m. the same day. Everyone was visibly beat, dead tired, and wished it was over, but Kip's cheeriness made us feel that if he could do it, so could we.

Sunday morning came way too quickly. Again, all through this long day of moving furniture, boxes, computers, flags, etc. Kip remained energetic, positive, and upbeat. About halfway through Sunday, as my stamina was totally depleted, I walked over to Kip and asked him to tell me the secret to remaining positive. His response was this: "If I let my job upset me, I will ruin my day."

This response was simple, concise, and profound. Even more curious was how inspiring and meaningful it was. If you dissect his sentence, among its component 12 words, five are either "I," "my," or "me." There is not a single "they," "them," "you," "it," "their," "those," or any reference to anyone or anything outside of himself as the cause of his emotional state. His sentence clearly demonstrated a core belief that *he, and only he* had full control over his attitude and emotions. He will not delegate his feelings to anyone. He will not give away his power over situations.

I found Kip's sentence moving and refreshing, probably because one of my pet peeves is people who believe they are the victims of circumstances. Those who blame others for everything that happens to them bother me. Kip was the exact opposite of this, which is why I found him so impressive and feel I learned a lesson from him. It appeared to me everyone on the courthouse team learned a lesson, too, as they worked harder and harder, following Kip's steadfast pace and inspirational attitude.

An important disclaimer: I understand life is not always fair and not everyone is dealt an even hand. I recognize race, gender, religious and financial discrimination exists in many ugly forms. People should speak up about such discrimination and not be viewed as complainers when they are unfairly treated. I was dealt a hand of privilege and I never experienced discrimination. My privilege was not one of wealth, nor a life without challenges, but simply being a white male in today's society, which makes life always easier than for those who face discrimination. I also had the privilege of having a loving mother who placed my receiving a good education above her own ability to afford a decent pair of shoes. I had the privilege of never going hungry. I grew up in a position of privilege, indeed.

A second lesson that has remained with me from this experience with Kip is to always remain curious and ask people to explain their reasons for doing something a certain way or having a specific opinion. If I had not asked Kip how he stayed so upbeat and positive, I would not have heard such powerful words from him. Asking direct or bold questions is not always easy for introverts like me. It is easier to live in our own heads, in our own world of ideas and thoughts, than to reach out and exchange ideas. While this approach to life may be easier, I now realize how much it limits life experiences. I have found my life greatly expanded when I break out of my introvert personality and reach out to others as I did with Kip.

I encourage you to think about all the self-talk going on inside your head. Become aware of that noise and chatter, and how much of it there is. In my case, when it starts to move toward the negative, I remind myself how nfluential the language in our head is to our mood. I try to move my mind chatter to a place of positive thinking. Halting "worst case scenario thinking" is not easy, but it is critical for peace of mind, happiness, and a richer life.

In case you're wondering how the court move ended, we succeeded—but it took every ounce of energy we had. Thanks to all involved, especially those who took on Kip's attitude, we accomplished the shift of buildings by late Sunday night, close to midnight. Monday morning the court was open for business, and the previously scheduled jury trial was held in our new courthouse. Everyone was beyond exhaustion, but we all had a tremendous feeling of accomplishment.

The other takeaway lesson I learned from that weekend is that we can receive many powerful, inspiring messages from all sources if we remain open to them. One does not have to read self-help books written by experts to learn inspirational lessons. You do not have to be sitting in some expensive conference listening to a professional speaker to take in provocative and potentially life-changing ideas. Rather, the most lasting lessons are often those observed in daily life and internalized through experiential learning, such as this courthouse moving weekend. When we remain open to what is unfolding around us, use our natural curiosity, and ask questions about other people's thinking, intentions, and motivations, it is amazing the insights we can add to our cookbook of positive thoughts and actions.

RECIPE REMINDERS FROM KIP THE MOVING GUY

- Self-talk is critical to how we think and behave. Kip's simple statement demonstrated how he accepted responsibility for what was going on in his life and paints the power of the internal language we use to talk to ourselves.

- Powerful messages can—and do—come from all places and people. Our challenge is remaining open to them with a curious mind.

- Avoid thinking you are a victim to your circumstances. If you do not like something happening in your life, work towards changing it.

Chapter 9

Do Not Judge the Success or Failure of Your
Actions Too Quickly

"Cooking is one failure after another, and that's how you finally learn."
–Julia Child

Have you ever felt like you failed at something, only to discover later you had not? Have you ever wished something had turned out differently, when you later discovered the end result was just as it was meant to be? Here is one such experience I encountered.

In my 30s, I was active in Valley Big Brothers in the Phoenix area. For those unfamiliar with the Big Brothers Big Sisters of America organization, it is a national nonprofit whose mission statement is the following: "Provide children facing adversity with strong and enduring professionally supported one-to-one relationships that change their lives for the better, forever."

If you read my chapter "Disconnecting the Dots," you probably understand why I felt a calling to be involved in this very important charity work that seeks to provide a stable adult role model for children who are lacking that in their lives. I was involved with Valley Big Brothers for approximately five or six years, mentoring four different little brothers over that period of time. Three of these matches were very successful and only ended because the family moved or the mother remarried, so the services of a Big Brother were no longer needed. However, one match did not end successfully, and this is my story of what I deemed to be my failure at the time.

To protect the anonymity of the young man, I will refer to him as Tom. Tom was 13 years old when Valley Big Brothers matched me with him. You begin a big brother-little brother relationship with a get-together at the charity's office. During this encounter you meet the youth and a decision is jointly made whether or not to proceed with the match. Tom and I seemed to hit it off at the initial meeting. I had been told he had some disciplinary problems in the past, but I thought I could still help this young man.

We hooked up once a week, usually on the weekend, for an outing. After a few months, it became apparent to me that our times together were frustrating for both of us. Tom seemingly had no sincere interest in having a Big Brother. I contacted my social worker at Valley Big Brothers and discussed the situation and options. If I recall correctly, Tom and I had a meeting with the social worker at the Big Brothers organization to process our status. Despite the rough patches, we agreed to try to make it work for another month or so.

Unfortunately, the situation did not improve, so with the aid of the social worker we all agreed to end the match. Ending a match of a Big Brother with a youth must be done with care and deliberateness to avoid making the young man feel abandoned, as some often are struggling with these emotions anyway. We tried our best to part on good terms.

For several years, I felt I had failed Tom. While I know I tried my best, and in several ways the odds were stacked against us from the start due to Tom already being a teenager and having some anger issues, I often wondered what I could have done differently to help him.

Then, much to my surprise, about three years after my last contact with Tom, he showed up in my office. He was now 16 years old and stopped in to ell me he was doing well in school and was very active in martial arts. Wow! was stunned. I had considered our friendship to be a complete failure when, n reality, I obviously made enough of a positive impression on Tom for him to want to circle back with me and let me know that things were going well in his ife. It was wonderful to see him, and we talked for a long time.

The lesson I took away from this experience is not to be so quick to judge your success or failure in relationships, as one never truly knows the impact you may have had on someone. Here I thought I had failed him, while Tom obviously had a different idea about our interactions.

Thinking about this deeply, it is also important to apply this same delay of judgment on other experiences in our lives. For example, I often jokingly tell people I liked eighth grade so much I decided to do it twice. Yes, true story. My first time through eighth grade was the year my father committed suicide over the Christmas holidays, and I was an emotional mess. I took out my anger about the situation by not caring about my studies. At the time, repeating the grade was tough enough for me, of course, and made me feel like a failure. However, thinking about it in hindsight, it gave me a wonderful opportunity to regroup after that traumatic year. I did very well my second time around eighth grade, which I believe set the stage for a successful experience in my remaining high school years.

I remain appreciative to this day for Tom taking the time to come by my office to update me on his life. I encourage you to think about those who had a positive impact on your life and to reach out to them to tell them so. It is likely they have no idea how you feel. I can think of several times I have wished after someone passed away that I had told that person what they meant to me. Today I now make a conscious effort to contact past mentors and others who had a positive influence in my life to tell them how they helped me. Every time I have done this, it has been a win-win for all involved. The person I am reaching out to is often surprised to hear my positive feedback so many years later and is always very appreciative, and I feel good about it as well.

RECIPE REMINDERS FOR DO NOT JUDGE THE SUCCESS OR FAILURE OF YOUR ACTIONS TOO QUICKLY

- We never know the true impact we have on others, so be careful not to assume failure too quickly.

- If someone had a positive influence on your life, make the time to tell them that while they are still alive, rather than in their eulogy.

- Make time to volunteer for charity work!

Chapter 10

Lessons About Worry from A Certified Mail Notice

"Recipes tell you nothing. Learning techniques is the key."

–Tom Colicchio

Have you ever opened your mailbox to find a notice that a certified letter awaits you, which must be picked up and signed for at the post office? You know that little green card the post office uses to notify you? Were you elated when you saw it or, like me, did you experience a sudden sense of panic at who might be sending you a certified letter and why?

In my case, I came home from work one evening, opened my mailbox at my condominium complex, and found such a notice. The post office had closed for the day so I had to wait until the morning to retrieve this certified letter. I immediately started worrying and spent a fitful, sleepless night fretting about the contents of this mysterious notice. The little voice inside my head just kept nagging on and on as I tossed and turned. Was someone suing me? Was it a letter from the IRS? Had I done something wrong?

Rationally I realized that, to my knowledge, I had done nothing wrong. There were no outstanding warrants for my arrest. There was no reason I could think of that someone would be suing me. And it was highly unlikely the library would be finally catching up to me for not returning that book when I was in the third grade. I was certain the statute of limitations had run out on that one! But despite my own reassurances that I could think of absolutely nothing I had done wrong, I could not imagine this letter bearing anything other than bad news.

Morning arrived and I made a beeline to the post office. I was first in line outside its doors 20 minutes before they opened, the little green card notice in hand. A postal employee finally appeared and unlocked the large brass doors of the inner office. I hesitantly approached the counter, presented the green postcard, and showed my identification. As the postal worker went to retrieve the letter, I could feel my pulse increasing and my palms getting sweaty. She handed me an envelope and I signed for it. Looking around to check out who might be watching me, I retreated to a dark back corner of the post office lobby to open it, afraid some total stranger might read it over my shoulder and find out what a terrible person I was.

I slid my thumb under the flap and gently tore at it, until the contents of the envelope were exposed. Inside was not a letter from a lawyer or a traffic ticket or an arrest warrant, but rather a note and a check made out to me for almost $1,000. What? I had no idea why someone was sending me a check in this amount. I unfolded the enclosed note, which explained an advertising error had been made about the air conditioning unit in the condominium I had purchased earlier that year. Apparently the one in my unit was not what had been advertised, and the legal agreement worked out with whoever raised this concern was either to offer all owners this check or to permit them to join in a class action lawsuit. As I could not care less about the type of air conditioning unit, and the one in my unit seemed to be working fine, I gladly cashed the check as soon as I could. Free money!

Going home, I realized I had spent all night worrying about this certified letter, yet it turned out to be good news: an unexpected windfall for me. My mind had tortured me for hours with every negative thought possible about myself when, in fact, I had no reason to go down that path. I had fabricated all kinds of wrongdoings I must have committed and nearly convinced myself the certified letter was proof positive I had been caught.

What I learned from this event was a valuable lesson for me and, I hope, serves as one for others: Strive to avoid jumping to negative conclusions and worst-case scenario thinking when presented with an uncertain situation. I use the words "strive to avoid" because I know reducing unnecessary worry is much easier said than done. As the opening quote for this chapter says, "Recipes tell you nothing. Learning techniques is the key." I translate this to mean the recipes in a self-help book aren't going to make you think positively; you need to develop techniques to think positively and practice them to make them part of your life.

I find it curious we often spend more time and energy practicing sports and hobbies than we do practicing the critical skills related to success in life. For instance, if you are preparing for a golf tournament, I would venture to guess you might go to the driving range several times to hit a couple buckets of balls to develop your swing. But if you are going into a difficult discussion at work or for a job interview, I doubt you found some friends to practice your discussion or interview techniques. In my view, just as we make time to practice our hobbies, we need to make time to practice the skills that keep us emotionally healthy—including reducing worry about things that are out of our control.

One of my favorite sayings about the need to practice is: "The harder I practice, the luckier I get." The origin of this saying is up in the air, as QuoteInvestigator.com credits it to a variety of golfers ranging from Gary Player to Arnold Palmer to Jerry Barber. But, no matter who said it, I love the ironic, teasing humor of this statement. It ultimately points out that our accomplishments derive from practice, not from luck. Indeed, more often than not a person's preparation has far more to do with a successful outcome than luck.

Here are a few ideas which with practice will hopefully help you along your journey toward worry-free—or at least less worried—thinking habits.

First, keep in mind a quote credited to American writer Terrance McKenna: "No one knows enough to worry." I love this quote as it serves as a reminder that regardless of how knowledgeable we think we are about a topic, there is still so much more to learn. What you may consider as fact today may prove to be incorrect in the future once you've learned more. If you start to worry about a situation, remind yourself of this quote and consider if you truly know enough about the situation or its likely outcome to close up your arteries about it.

Second, I suggest you practice mindfulness to reduce your tendency to worry. There are many techniques to achieve mindfulness, from a full-blown meditation practice to just relaxing and allowing yourself to have a short period of deep breathing. I have tried the former but, like some people, I was not successful in building meditation into my daily routine. But I have been easily able to work into my routine a few minutes of deep breathing each day. Calming the body and the mind for even two minutes can work wonders on you. You become more centered and mindful of what is truly important in your life.

Let me acknowledge that even a brief pause to do deep breathing every day took me a great deal of practice to turn it into a regular daily habit. At first, I felt like a complete failure whenever I tried doing it, as my mind would immediately wander to whatever was bothering me. I would begin breathing deeply and relaxing, but within minutes my mind would drift back to all the worries and negative thoughts I had that day. However, after significant practice, I became increasingly adept at letting go and not focusing on my worries. I began appreciating that the thoughts running through my mind while doing the deep breathing exercises were there for a reason and were meant to be. Rather than getting frustrated about these thoughts, accepting them made it easier to let go of them so I could get back to focusing on my breathing.

Third, have a sense of humor about life. Being able to laugh is an excellent way to reduce worrying and is critical to your emotional health when facing a stressful situation. I have seen examples, as I trust you have as well, of people damaging their career when they lost their sense of humor and started taking themselves too seriously. This is not to say work and relationships should not be taken seriously, just that we need to keep everything in perspective and find ways to laugh about situations whenever possible.

Fourth, linked closely with having a sense of humor to reduce needless worrying, I suggest you find ways to be playful. If you think about it, all of us grew up as children loving to play, but as adults we abandoned it and consider it childish. If you see a child skipping through a mall, you would think nothing of it. But if your doctor skipped into the examination room, you would likely start Googling medical malpractice attorneys. When I write my next book, the title may be, *When Did We Stop Skipping?* We need to keep that childlike sense of wonder alive, regardless of what age we are.

I am not suggesting you go around skipping everywhere to show you are playful. There are oodles of other ways to be playful. Even work tasks can be turned into a game. For example, years ago a coworker and I had to count through thousands of index cards every month to prepare various statistical reports. It was super boring work, taking at least a full day. We found it was more efficient to have two people do it together—one to look through the cards and call out the data while the other wrote down the information. (It feels so archaic writing about this, as I am sure that job of counting index cards is now completely automated!)

One day we decided to turn our task into a game. The person reading off the data had to see how fast he could go through a stack of the cards. We started timing each other, and all of a sudden we had an exciting, light-hearted, competitive game going on. It made the work much more fun—and we even became more efficient at doing it.

I have also found making a game of writing my daily to-do list is a way to be more playful. I group a number of small tasks together and then give myself an arbitrary goal of getting them all done by a certain hour. It's like a gaming challenge I give myself to test my own abilities to get stuff done, not all that different than what kids do today playing video games and trying to beat their best score. Being more playful and finding humor in situations takes away much of the worry about any task at hand, as it is hard to be worried and have fun at the same time.

Finally, an effective technique to remind yourself to strive to avoid worry is to create a short phrase or a symbol that you bring to mind any time you feel worry coming on. The phrase I developed derives from my certified mail notice experience. Any time I encounter an unknown situation with an uncertain outcome, I say to myself "green card," reminding myself of that little green certified mail notice I found in my mailbox. Just saying this phrase keeps me from over-thinking a situation and it humorously reminds me of the time when I worried all night only to have money fall from the sky.

As with any skill set, practice and repetition are required to master this key phrase technique and have it work for you. Try it for a few days. Find a phrase that reminds you of a situation in which you worried yourself to death for no reason. See the humor in how you worried and then everything turned out fine. Then, the next time you begin to worry, repeat your phrase over and over again. Say it as many times as necessary to help you see the futility of worrying about something you ultimately cannot control—which, come to think of it, is most things in life.

A last note: I do not mean to infer that all worrying is bad, as that could imply I am encouraging you to suppress your feelings. Worrying about some situations is necessary, as it is a reflection of your feelings. Feelings are what make us human. Trying to suppress your emotions can cause psychological harm and even physical harm. There are things in life that warrant worry, like caring about a loved one's health, a challenging situation at work, your family, and so on. But what I am talking about is trying to minimize worrying about things for which you have no control over the outcome. I am thinking especially about events or circumstances for which you truly have no idea if the outcome will be good or bad—like receiving a certified mail notice in your mailbox. Instead, strive to look at every opportunity and challenge as a learning opportunity, and practice the tools I gave you in this chapter to avoid needless, circular worrying that usually leads to worst-case scenario thinking. Spend your life dishing up positive food for thought, rather than stewing in the negative.

RECIPE REMINDERS FOR LESSONS ABOUT WORRY FROM A CERTIFIED MAIL NOTICE

- Work on reducing or eliminating worrying about minor things in life, especially things over which you have absolutely no control.
- Develop a catchphrase or symbol from a personal story to remind you to stay positive. Repeat this phrase over and over again if you start to move into worst-case scenario thinking about a circumstance or upcoming event.
- Keep a sense of humor and work every day to find ways to be playful.
- And remember to practice all of the above! Practice may not make perfect, in this case, but it certainly cannot hurt, and will likely help you in your quest to reduce worrying.

Chapter 11

Dashboard Bagels

"Food is not just eating energy. It's an experience."

– Guy Fieri

Years ago my wife and I elected to move to Las Vegas where, in the summer months, when the sun crests over Sunrise Mountain east of the city, there is nothing gentle about it. It is like opening a blast furnace door in your face, a feeling I know all too well from having labored in an aluminum foundry as a summer job during my high school years. While not quite metal-melting temperatures, thermometers in Vegas often read in the mid-90s in the early morning and skyrocket to 115 by midday—enough to turn humans into puddles of sweaty flesh. Yes, this is where we choose to live, the word "choose" being the operative term of intentionality, as I will explain.

The intense summer heat usually starts in May and can last well into the end of September. As summer approaches, radio and television stations often have contests in which people guess the day and hour when the temperature will first hit 100 degrees. As soon as the searing heat becomes a daily reality, many people start to complain as if they think they might wake up one morning to winter. Wherever you go, it is common to hear comments such as: "This heat is terrible," or "I hate it here in Las Vegas," and, of course, the threat of threats, "I am going to move away."

But not me. No, I do not complain about the summer heat in Vegas as this is dashboard bagel season! It's the time of year when I transform into one of the most innovative bakers in the world. What's amazing is that I didn't go to the Cordon Bleu or some fancy pastry school in Paris to learn my baking skills. Nope, I learned them right here in the desert heat of Vegas.

Allow me to share my inspirational recipe for dashboard bagels. Some of the processes in these directions are easy, but others require a significant life adjustment that, I believe, is worth learning.

Here is the hardest part for many readers: you have to be willing to live someplace where it gets really, really hot in the summer—a location with abundant sunshine. When I say "willing," I am referring to having an attitude-adjusting perspective that you totally, unconditionally accept the heat. I mean you agree not to complain about it, or threaten to move away from it, because having this heat is vital to the success of this recipe.

This degree of acceptance is not a piece of cake for many people (ah, that's another recipe idea: baking a cake dashboard-bagel style!). Depending on where you live, it may require you to move somewhere in the southwest United States, like Arizona, New Mexico, Utah, or Nevada—especially if you like your bagels crispy. If it hits 90 to 100 where you live, you'll probably be okay though the recipe calls for more like 105 to 110 degrees.

Undertaking two of the recipe instructions is much easier. Go out and purchase some bagels—any type or flavor you prefer. I opt for whole wheat but that's my taste; you can get whatever flavor of bagel appeals to you. Do not eat them immediately (okay, you can have one if you must, but save the majority for this recipe). Place the bagels in a plastic bag and freeze them.

The third phase of the recipe for dashboard bagels is possibly the hardest s it may require more discipline than you currently have. But I promise the eward is far greater than simply cooking up the recipe.

Next, you must go out and join a health club if you are not already in one. If you are, great! Just follow the next direction, too.) After joining the club, et in the habit of driving to the gym where you will work out for at least an our before a meal. Just because I cook my bagels for breakfast does not mean ou have to. If you want yours for lunch or dinner, that will work fine, too, as ong as it is scorching hot outside your car. Be sure to bring one or two frozen agels with you in a plastic baggie and put it on the front passenger seat so you von't forget about them. (If you aren't that hungry, or don't want the calories, ne bagel is enough, of course.) If you normally cannot eat a bagel without utter or cream cheese, bring those along too, but store them in a cooler in the ar.

This next instruction is fairly simple. Upon arrival at your health club, park our car so that your windshield is (or will be) facing the sun when it comes up if it is not already up). Then grab the bag of bagels and freely toss them onto he dashboard as you leave your car. Be sure to toss the bag with wild abandon, s that is the fun of it.

Now go enjoy your (minimum) hour-long workout. If you spent the full our in your gym, you will be amazed when you return to your car. The reviously frozen bagels will be sitting there on your dashboard, fully cooked o perfection—nice and warm in the middle.

Given how famished you will be after your strenuous workout, the next tep will be pretty easy and come to you naturally. Open the bag, eat, and enjoy!

If you choose to become a dashboard bagel baker you will discover, as I lid, that you will no longer have any objection to your area's summer weather. While others are complaining about the heat, you no longer have to join them as you can celebrate dashboard bagel season. Like me, you will look forward to the awe of chomping down on a perfectly heated bagel after a workout that helped slim down and tone your body.

We make many choices in our lives. One of them is about where we reside. No one is forced to live anywhere, especially where the summer sun will fry your bare feet in a matter of seconds, should you venture onto the gooey pavement. When my family opted to move to Las Vegas, I knew it would be very hot in the summer. Rather than complain like many of my friends, I elect to celebrate by cooking bagels on the dashboard of my car.

Obviously, you do not really have to move to a hellish climate to put the lesson of this recipe into practice. It's not just about where you live. The lesson in dashboard bagels is bigger than that—and I hope it is obvious by now: we each have a choice over how we react to different circumstances.

I find it very sad, if not heartbreaking, to see so many people go through their lives in a miserable state of mind, feeling like victims, like they have no control over their situation. I am not sure why this is the case, but I have a theory. While unhappy in their current situation, some people are fearful of making any change, as the uncertainty of what the change will bring is more controlling than the possible benefits of making the change. In other words, the pain of their life situation is not severe enough for someone to want to change their situation or attitude toward it.

Les Brown, a wonderful motivational speaker, tells a story that relates to what I am talking about. I heard him tell this story and immediately saw its correlation to my dashboard bagels. It goes like this: There was a young man walking down the street who happened to see an old man sitting on his porch. Next to the old man was his dog, who was whining and whimpering. The young man asked the old man: "What's wrong with your dog" The old man said: "He's

ying on a nail." The young man asked: "Laying on a nail? Well, why doesn't
e get up?" The old man replied: "It's not hurting badly enough."[1]

Some people complain about situations in their lives but do not do anything
bout them because, like the dog on the nail, it does not hurt badly enough yet
o move. They suffer their internal pain as they do not respect that they have a
hoice to do some other action or behave some other way. They remain willing
o live with this attitude for many possible reasons.

I asked previously why anyone would choose a life of unhappiness and
displeasure when we can choose happiness instead. I am not saying that it is
easy to change or that life is always fair, or that people should not grieve loss,
feel pain, or express and experience sorrow when tragic things happen. For
sure, we all have losses and moments of sadness or dissatisfaction with
challenging situations in our lives. Suppressing your feelings in these situations
can cause much more harm to the psyche than feeling and processing the true
emotions accompanying the circumstance.

Of course, you do not need to move to a new city or start an exercise
program to change your attitude. What is necessary is changing the way you
perceive the situation, which is usually much easier than actually changing
whatever is sparking your stress.

I use the bagel analogy as a visual reminder that I can repeat over and over
again any time I find myself moving toward negative thinking about anything.
Having this reminder is a good way for me to stop and think deeper and more
carefully about the situation at hand so I make a conscious decision about how
I want to react. The visualization of me throwing my bagels on the dashboard

---

[1] Brown, Les. *Live Your Dreams.* Morrow, 1994.

helps me reframe the problem so that I can react in my best interest and in the best interest of those around me.

I encourage you to find your own personal example, your own dashboard bagel reminder, and to practice thinking about that cue whenever you are feeling trapped or uninspired. And, most importantly, remember this image tossing your bagels on your dashboard is also a symbolic gesture of tossing your problems to the wind.

RECIPE REMINDERS FOR DASHBOARD BAGELS

- You have a choice over your reaction to any situation.
- Viewing something or someone in a positive light may require practice and self-introspection.
- Work on differentiating what is truly worth being concerned about versus what can easily be shrugged off as a minor inconvenience.
- Find ways to turn challenges into games—like cooking bagels on your dashboard, rather than complaining about the heat!

Chapter 12

Swim On, John

"I'm not asking any of you to make drastic changes to every single one of your recipes or to totally change the way you do business. But what I am asking is that you consider reformulating your menu in pragmatic and incremental ways to create healthier versions of the foods that we all love."

–Michelle Obama

I f there are noble ways to die, throwing yourself on top of a person standing next to you in line when gunfire breaks out certainly must be one of them. Admittedly, knowing the exact sequence of events when a mass shooting breaks out is often impossible. However, this is what I have been told my friend, the late Honorable John M. Roll, did outside a Safeway supermarket in Tucson, Arizona, on January 8, 2011. If you recall, that was the morning when Jared Loughner opened fire on an unsuspecting crowd in an attempt to assassinate U.S. Representative Gabrielle Giffords at a "Congress on Your Corner" event she was conducting. Judge Roll was shot in the back and died. The manner in which he left this life is testament to his selflessness. But I write to share different insights I learned from Judge Roll through our friendship; lessons of balance and wellness.

I created this painting, titled "Swim On John," as a tribute to my friend.
will explain the symbolism embedded in this painting shortly, but let me begin
by telling you more about Judge Roll and why I speak of him often as an
example of someone who truly knew how to keep everything in perspective
while living a busy and demanding life.

John McCarthy Roll was born in Pittsburgh, Pennsylvania on February 8
1947. His family moved to Tucson, Arizona when he was a child. He received
his undergraduate and law degree from the University of Arizona; he also held
a Master of Laws from the University of Virginia School of Law.

Judge Roll held several positions as an attorney in Tucson prior to being
appointed as a state court judge in Pima County, Arizona in 1987. He served in
that role for four years, after which President George H.W. Bush appointed him

o fill a vacancy on the United States District Court for the District of Arizona in 1991. He was in this position until his untimely and senseless death in 2011.

What did Judge Roll do that fateful Saturday morning before he was murdered? I do not know for sure, but permit me to speculate as I know well what he did almost every other morning. The first thing he likely did was to attend Catholic Mass, his practice every Saturday and Sunday morning. There were actually many times in his life when he attended Catholic mass every day! Then, assuming he followed his normal morning routine, he swam laps for a full mile.

According to Judge Roll's loving wife, Maureen, what he did next that morning was to go over to Congresswoman Gifford's event to thank her for supporting his court's efforts to obtain additional judges. He told Maureen that he'd be back in a few minutes. She never saw him alive again.

After the shooting in Tucson, Chief Justice of the United States Supreme Court John Roberts issued this statement:

The violence in Arizona today has senselessly taken five lives and inflicted tragic loss on dedicated public servants and their families. We in the judiciary have suffered the terrible loss of one of our own. Chief Judge John Roll was a wise jurist who selflessly served Arizona and the nation with great distinction, as attorney and judge, for more than 35 years. I express my deepest condolences to his wife Maureen and his children, as well as the other victims and their families. Chief Judge Roll's death is a somber reminder of the importance of the rule of law and the sacrifices of those who work to secure it.

I am blessed to claim Judge Roll as one of the most inspiring friends I had the pleasure of knowing. Our initial contact was in a professional capacity, as we both worked in the federal court system. But shortly after we met, we discovered we both shared early morning lap swimming as our preferred form of exercise, and we became early morning lap swim buddies.

Although I lived in Las Vegas and Judge Roll lived in Tucson, we would be together three or four times a year at work-related meetings. Prior to these gatherings, we would connect with each other and one of us would research where to swim laps. Sometimes our hotel pool was long enough and open early enough for us to get in a workout before most people got out of bed. (I trust the statute of limitations has expired on this confession, but if the hotel pool was long enough to swim laps but was not open early enough, we had been known to climb over the fencing. Please do not share this little secret, as it is not my intention to tarnish Judge Roll's stellar reputation.) Other times, we discovered a nearby YMCA or fitness center to satisfy our mutual early morning passion. In addition to enjoying having a friend with whom to burn some calories, I have fond memories of the discussions Judge Roll and I often had after our swim.

What inspired me most about my lap-swimming partner was that even with the incredible responsibility of being Chief Judge at one of the nation's busiest federal courts, he still took time to practice his spirituality and to exercise every morning. Think about how often you have heard people exclaim "I'm too busy to work out!" or "If I only had more than 24 hours in a day, I would have time to do... *[fill in the blank]."* My response would be: "Everyone has only 24 hours in a day, and if my friend, Judge Roll, could make time to stay healthy by swimming a mile every morning, I think most of us can find time to squeeze in some exercise."

People I know often talk about finding balance between work demands and their other interests, such as family, exercising, hobbies, etc. However, my observation is that very few people actually create this balance in their life. They simply lament not having it, without ever even trying. Judge Roll was the rare example of someone who figured it out.

72

Whenever I think of Judge Roll, two very special, humorous memories come to mind. The first took place when he was in my home city of Las Vegas on business, though I did not know it. I had just finished my laps at the YMCA and was walking around the locker room in my birthday suit when I looked across and spotted Judge Roll in a similar situation. I enthusiastically yelled out "Hi, Judge Roll!" Although I trust he was pleased to see me, I am equally confident that is the last place and time he expected to hear a greeting called out to him.

Another fun memory occurred at a meeting we were both attending near the ocean. I met up with Judge Roll and he asked if I had some ideas about where we were going to swim. I smiled and pointed to the beautiful, calm, blue Pacific Ocean beyond the beach. He looked at me with wonder and asked, "Really, can we swim out there?" I made some smart aleck retort, like: "Is it water, isn't it?"

We proceeded to do our laps together in that enormous salty pool nature had created. Judge Roll was like a little kid enjoying swimming long distances in the ocean for the first time. Every day he wore a huge smile on his face, and one could sense his childlike wonderment at how much fun it was to do distance swimming in open waters. He never lost his passion for swimming or for anything else he did in life! I learned a fun fact when sharing this chapter with Maureen Roll. She informed me that on her first date with Judge Roll, he took her to a public swimming pool. His love for swimming went way back to courting his soon-to-be bride.

Now that you have a better understanding of my relationship with Judge Roll, let me circle back and explain my painting. I created it for Judge Roll's widow. (Note: A color version of the painting is on the back cover.) Its bright, varied, and vibrant colors represent the glowing spirit with which Judge Roll lived his life, his wide-ranging interests, and his vibrant personality that lives on today. The water depicts the gift of life, and the peaceful rolling waves reflect the Judge's calmness and consistency. I painted the bright rays of sun shining through, just as did his positive attitude. The dove symbolizes the sign of peace, as he was a man of peace. And, lastly, the swim goggles being carried off into the sunset by the dove represent our shared passion for early morning lap swimming and a reminder of his commitment to living a well-balanced life.

The main lesson I learned from Judge Roll was about how we all can create balance in life if we strive to. He tended to professional obligations in an exemplary manner while at the same time making time to take care of himself spiritually and physically. As I told Judge Roll's wife, Maureen, at his memorial service in Tucson, every time I put on my swim goggles for my early morning workout, I think of Judge Roll and say a silent prayer in his honor. I am grateful to have known him and to be able to call him my friend. I lament the tragedy of his death, gunned down for no reason by a crazed man.

Look again at the opening quote by Michelle Obama in this chapter. "What I am asking is that you consider reformulating your menu in pragmatic and incremental ways to create healthier versions of the foods that we all love." To honor Judge Roll's legacy, I have a similar request. What I ask of you is that you reformulate your daily menu in pragmatic and incremental ways to create a healthy balance in your life. Then you, too, could swim through life with the same balance and passion as my early morning lap-swimming friend, the Honorable John M. Roll.

RECIPE REMINDERS FROM SWIM ON, JOHN

Strive to find a healthy balance in your busy life. Yes, take your work responsibilities very seriously, but also make time to take care of yourself emotionally and physically.

Never take a loved one for granted. The morning of January 8, 2011, Judge Roll and Mrs. Roll had no idea they would not see each other again when he left the house for "a few minutes." Do not leave a loved one or friend with anything other than what you would want to be your last interaction.

Live life with a passion and zest.

STATEMENT FROM MAUREEN ROLL

The Honorable John M. Roll

John was a wonderful husband, father to our three sons, and papa to our grandchildren. He was compassionate and fair-minded in life and as a judge. When you continue to hear from people who knew him, as well as total strangers, who say, "John was a very good man," I think it speaks volumes about him. He is dearly loved and never forgotten.

Chapter 13

Let Me Be Brave in The Attempt

"In my food world, there is no fear or guilt, only joy and balance."

–Ellie Kriege

Have you ever coached youth sports? If so, I hope you had a wonderful time. Unfortunately, I did not have a positive experience while coaching my son's soccer team when he was six years old. I went into this new adventure with high expectations, and my interactions with the children were wonderful.

The parents, on the other hand, were not so much fun. I encountered perhaps all the horror stories one hears about parents misbehaving at youth sporting events. The children I was coaching were in kindergarten or first grade. Despite this young age, a couple parents used stop watches at every practice and gave me an earful if their child did not get as much playing time as did the other athletes.

Of course I did my best to make sure all children got equal time and attention, but I did not have a timer on me. I also had parents screaming at their children, yelling at the referees, and getting into arguments with parents from the other teams. One season of this was the end of my coaching youth soccer, though not the end of my coaching career.

Around this same time, my amazing spouse was coordinating communit
outreach efforts at the church we were attending and arranged for our group t
assist with a Special Olympics swimming competition. While I had n
experience in working with children and adults with different learning abilities
this was a very pleasant change for me compared to coaching youth soccer. A
these athletes were striving to win, and some of the parents exhibited
competitive spirit themselves, but overall this experience was much more abou
celebrating what is right with the world. It was not about trying to win at a
costs and finding fault with those volunteering to assist in the sporting event.

I enjoyed this day of volunteering so much that shortly thereafter I reache
out to the local Special Olympics office to see if they might need coaches fo
other sporting events. As it turned out, the stars aligned perfectly for me; the
were just getting geared up with a soccer program, and I was afforded th
opportunity to coach a Special Olympics soccer team. This was 17 years ag
and I have now been coaching the same team since then. I am pleased to shar
some of lessons I've learned from this activity.

If you are not familiar with Special Olympics, their mission statemen
reads: "[...] to provide year-round sports training and athletic competition in
variety of Olympic-type sports for children and adults with intellectua
disabilities, giving them continuing opportunities to develop physical fitness
demonstrate courage, experience joy and participate in a sharing of gifts, skill
and friendship with their families, other Special Olympics athletes and th
community."

Special Olympics are for athletes of all ages. Over the years, my socce
players have ranged in age from seven to 60 years old. Their ability levels rang
as well, with some being able to play competitive soccer games while others d
best practicing skills rather than playing an actual game. Regardless of ability
my goal in coaching these athletes is threefold: first, to make sure everyone ha

un; second, to help them develop soccer skills; and last, to demonstrate and each good sportsmanship and respect. These goals are not ranked in order, as hey are all important, but if I had to rank them, I would put teaching good portsmanship and respect first.

At the beginning of each season, I always hold a discussion with the thletes about the rules and boundaries of practice sessions. I ask them what ur rules should be. I am heartened that, each year, one of the athletes will bring p not making fun of the other athletes as a guiding principle. We then discuss ow it is okay to laugh with another member of the team, but never to laugh at hat person. We also cover rules such as no name calling, following nstructions, and, of course, making sure we all have fun.

A story comes to mind about respect and good sportsmanship. In fact, I hink the Special Olympics athlete handled the situation better than I did. My eam practices every Saturday morning for ten weeks in the fall at a large open ield at a local park. We often wind up sharing the field with others; it may be group of people and canines doing dog training, a youth football team, or ome other activity. Usually there are no problems, but once we experienced an ssue with a group of adult men playing football at the other end of the field.

It seemed like just an informal pickup game between guys ranging from 20 o 35 years old. They had family members, including small children, present to vatch them play. Throughout their game, in their manly enthusiasm, the "F-omb" was loudly screamed during or after almost every play. Every time this profanity was yelled, one of my female athletes (who was around 35 years old nd who lived in a group-home setting) would turn and yell something like this t them: "Hey, I heard that. Stop cursing." At one point she actually yelled at hem: "There are women and children over here, stop cursing!"

Even as I write about this, years after the event, I am not thrilled with the vay I tried to handle it. I recall mentioning to my athlete that I agreed with her—what they were doing was highly inappropriate. And in an attempt to avoid a conflict with the football players, I encouraged my athlete to try to ignore the rude and offensive comments. What I did not do was approach the men and ask them to tone it down. I thought about it, but I saw that they had close to 50 people, including their spectators, and I was a total of one—a bit outnumbered! In hindsight, being braver sitting at my desk typing this story, truly wish I had approached them and said something.

The takeaway from this story is obvious: a Special Olympics athlete had a better sense of right and wrong than did this group of grown men. A second takeaway, however, is that I should have taken a risk and approached the men and asked them to stop the foul language for everyone's sake.

As I said, our goal is to have fun —and we do at every practice! For example, at the beginning of each season, I challenge the athletes to invent our team name. We have been everything from the Jaguars to the Flying Monkeys. The only time I overruled their choice was when one of them recommended our name be The Las Vegas Strippers, and all the athletes quickly agreed. While have a great deal of latitude when coaching, I had the feeling that the Special Olympics office would have been a bit shocked when I informed them of this team name.

I had a fun experience with one of my athletes at my place of employment several years ago. As with many federal government buildings, this one was cleaned by a nonprofit organization that hires men and women with intellectual disabilities to do the janitorial work. I believe there is a regulation that requires the General Services Administration—the landlord for federal agencies—to offer these contracts to such organizations before hiring a for-profit company. Such groups cleaned all three federal courthouses where I worked in my professional career. I always enjoyed my interactions with the cleaning crews.

So, one day, imagine my surprise when I entered one of our courtrooms in the evening to discover one of my Special Olympic athletes cleaning the space. It was wonderful hearing him say: "Hi, Coach Lance." As if my ego was not big enough already, being called Coach in my place of employment was a delight.

Another humorous story of coaching the Special Olympics athletes is the following. One year I had an assistant coach in his mid-twenties—a handsome, well-muscled young man who obviously lifted weights regularly. I cannot recall his name, but for the purpose of this story let's call him Bill. We were sitting at a picnic table during a break one morning and an athlete who has been with me on the team since I started coaching said the following: "Bill, he is very handsome. And Lance, he is very old!" What?! Here I am, minding my own business, and I get slammed by one of my athletes. We all had a good laugh.

I also derive joy from providing the parents and caregivers of the Special Olympians an opportunity to relax, chat, and bond with each other during our practices. They show up with their lawn chairs, sit together in the shade, and spend two hours watching and engaging in conversation with each other. I always sense how much they appreciated a well-earned respite to have a breather before returning to providing loving care for their child or person for whom they assist.

Like most things in life, coaching these athletes is not always all laughter and fun; it comes with heart-wrenching moments as well. For example, I had an athlete who stopped mid-field while dribbling the ball and started to cry because he missed his mom who had passed away many years before. One morning, another athlete told me he was taking classes to learn how to be more independent because his grandmother, his only family member and caregiver, would be going to heaven soon and he needed to learn to live on his own. I learned more from those moments than I did from the light-hearted ones.

Circling back to the title of this chapter, "Let Me Be Brave in the Attempt" is part of the motto of the Special Olympics. The full saying is: "Let me win but if I can't win, let me be brave in the attempt." Athletes recite this meaningful pledge at the beginning of every Special Olympics official competition. These athletes are brave in the attempt in many ways. They are brave in the attempt when giving 100% effort. They are brave in the attempt when they run hard ignoring physical challenges. They are brave in the attempt when they call out others for using inappropriate language. They are brave when they stop to help another athlete up off the ground. They are brave in the attempt when they strive to be more independent. The world would be a better place if we all strove to be brave in the attempt, like these inspiring athletes.

RECIPE REMINDERS FOR LET ME BE BRAVE IN THE ATTEMPT

- Celebrate what is right in the world; make time to volunteer, and teach others to have fun.

- As the opening quote to the chapter says: "In the food world, there is no fear or guilt, only joy and balance." The same can be true in all that you do.

- Get outside your comfort zone; lessons can be learned from anywhere at any time.

STATEMENT FROM KATHY TREANTS, MOTHER OF BRIANNE TREANTS, WHO HAS PLAYED ON LANCE WILSON'S SOCCER TEAM SINCE HE STARTED COACHING

Brianne said she thinks of you more of a friend and someone who can make er laugh. She knows you know when she says you are her "best coach" that ill only last until the next Special Olympic event and the next "best coach."

For me, having known Lance for 17 years (give or take), my takeaway is le respect and difference one volunteer can make in not just the athletes but le caregivers and families as well. As a parent, it is not unusual for me to hear omeone say involvement with Special Olympics has had a profound effect on hem. I see it in a very different way: that someone is so generous with their ime and knowledge will take the opportunity of giving a parent a little break, f only for 90 minutes once a week; that someone will respect the family enough o ask questions about how best to work with their child; and that someone is ip to the risk every week of not knowing what that week might hold out for hem from their usually uninhibited athletes!

Chapter 14

Highway One *Domestique,* And Other Pedaling Proverbs

"When you meet someone, ask about what hobby they have, not what they do. People always ask me about cooking, but I prefer to talk about tennis or boxing."

–Wolfgang Puck

Several years ago I fell in love with the sport of cycling. I love riding bikes. I love custom handmade bikes. I love organized cycling events. I love my local cycling community.

I love watching and following professional cycling. I love teaching kids how to ride at bike safety events. I love everything about bicycles. And I have learned several fun and valuable lessons from this passion of mine, divided into three categories: giving back, testing one's self, and saying yes to new adventures.

GIVING BACK

What is a "Highway 1 *Domestique*"? You may guess that the term *domestique* is French, meaning *servant*. What this has to do with biking may surprise you. In professional team cycling, such as you might know from the Tour de France, a *domestique* is a teammate whose role is to support one or more stronger riders on the same team. The *domestique* has no intention of winning the race; his or her sole job on the team is to support the leader who has the best chance of winning.

Domestiques are still strong cyclists who have likely won many races in their career. But in a specific race, their role is to help another rider win. They accomplish this in several ways. They may drop back to the team car to fetch water for the other riders on their team. They may ride at the front of the team for long periods of time to provide "drafting"—advantageous aerodynamics for teammates behind them. They may give their bike to the stronger rider, should that person have a mechanical problem. And, finally, *domestiques* on a professional cycling team can surround their strongest rider to keep him or her safe.

I gave myself the name "Highway 1 *Domestique*" for a week a few years back. No, I was not on a pro bike racing team. Rather, I rode the *domestique* slot for a group of teenagers on a weeklong ride. We were on Highway 1, the gorgeous curvy road that runs nearly the entire length of the California coast with its amazing views of the Pacific Ocean. We started in Palo Alto and ended in Santa Barbara—a distance of about 300 miles.

My job was to keep the teenagers safe as we rode. If the bike lane was wide enough for two riders to be side by side, I would always make sure the teenager was on the inside of the bike path, furthest away from traffic approaching from behind. I would also keep a constant eye out for approaching traffic and

ossible dangers, like obstacles in the road. I focused my attention on the
eenagers' riding style. Were they paying enough attention to their
urroundings? Were they practicing safe riding skills? If not, I gently corrected
hem.

Serving in this capacity provided me with some food for thought over the
ears. The first was how much joy I derived from riding to help others, rather
han doing it for myself. At home, on my daily rides, I ride for my own exercise
nd my own enjoyment. This trip was just the opposite as I was riding to ensure
thers had a good time and stayed safe.

The second insight I realized was how much I enjoyed the very relaxed
ace of this ride. No one was racing. No one was in a hurry. No one was trying
o beat someone else up a hill. This was a very different experience for me and
truly enjoyed it. And I have attempted to carry that more relaxed attitude
oward riding to this day. Well, most of the time, anyway.

Cycling is a sport that often aims to give back by having most organized
ides linked to a charity. One charity ride in which I participated was to raise
noney for medical bills for a little girl fighting for her life battling cancer.
Vhile waiting for the ride to start, I saw a local mechanic with his bike stand
et up and his tools out offering free maintenance. I coasted over to him and
ueried if the family of the little girl asked him to come to provide this service.
Ie replied, "No, I just saw it was happening and I wanted to help." The world
vould be a better place if we followed this mechanic's example and showed up
vanting to help.

I have seen such volunteerism occur at many biking events. For instance, I
vas the founder of a ride to raise money for the Special Olympics Nevada. As
wrote in the chapter titled "Let Me Be Brave in the Attempt," I have a strong
ove and appreciation for Special Olympics athletes. Years ago, when I was on
n advisory board for Special Olympics Nevada, I suggested a bike ride to raise

funds for the organization. This turned into an event called Pedal to the Meda which had six very successful years raising funds and building awareness of th needs of this wonderful organization.

When I first suggested the event, I was naive about the work it takes to pu on a cycling event! I had no idea about how much effort went into the details planning the route, obtaining permits, insurance, food during rest stops, rentin port-a-potties, scheduling of volunteers for registration, and on and on. Initially I also thought we would get maybe 50 or so riders to participate each year. Bu we started out at 200 riders registered the first year—already a shock to me— and climbed to over 600 riders by the sixth year! This never could hav happened without the incredible help of many volunteers.

Each year several Special Olympics athletes were on hand to assist with th event and to cheer for the riders. One year, at the post-ride lunch offered t every rider and participant after the ride, I noticed a few Special Olympic athletes approaching a table filled with some of the most "elite" riders in town As in many sports, there are always some people who take themselves to seriously and think they are better than others because of their abilities Fortunately, these riders are the exception in the sport, not the norm. The rider at this table were, in my opinion, among this small minority, and, I wa concerned they might shun the Special Olympics athletes. I had a queasy feeling in my stomach, as I did not think this pending interaction would en well.

To my delight, I was dead wrong. The riders quickly became engaged with the Special Olympics athletes. I listened to their friendly banter. The cyclist were asking the Special Olympics athletes about sports they played and thei other interests. This warmed my heart and changed my thinking about thes cyclists. It is this kind of generosity and compassion I love about the cyclin community. I am reminded of Wayne Dyer's quote: "Change the way you look things, and the things you look at change." This observation permanently changed my opinion of these elite cyclists, for the better.

TESTING ONE'S SELF

Riding bikes can also be a great way to challenge yourself to new personal heights. There's a ride I've participated in twice called the "Death Ride." This grueling 129-mile ride over five mountain passes in central California calls one's sanity into question. This area is referred to as the "California Alps," as its majestic mountain peaks rise to over 10,000 feet in altitude. If you complete this ride, not only do you ride 129 miles, but you also climb 15,000 feet in one day.

An interesting lesson I learned from the two times I did this ride is that I had a much easier time completing the ride the first time than the second time. Four years separated these two events, so you might be tempted to think my aging legs were the cause, but I discovered a more influential factor was my attitude about finishing. The first time, I was fully dedicated to finishing; I was dead set on challenging myself to complete the ride. The second time, though, I found I did not care as much if I finished. I even told many people that before the ride, letting them know I had nothing to prove now that I had already done it once. In my mind, and out loud to others, I said I might even stop after the third or fourth mountain pass. In the end, I did complete the second ride, but it became very clear to me I made it much harder on myself than the first time by not having the right attitude. I had done the same amount of training, was in the same physical shape, and the weather was similar. The only difference was my passion for completing the ride. This experience bolstered my long held belief that attitude truly does make a difference in your efforts in life.

The impact attitude can have was also reinforced one Saturday afternoo. as I was coasting on a beautiful, tree covered, back country road outside o Solvang, California. This was a century ride, meaning we were biking 10 miles in one day. It was an organized event for which the bikers had paid t participate.

I was rolling past rich, green pastures dotted with cattle and looking at th rolling hills in the distance. I wished time could just stop at that very momen as life seemed perfect. Just as I was in that peaceful state of mind, two rider passed me and I overheard one say to the other, "I just can't wait to get thi over with."

Wow! Here I was having the time of my life amidst some of the mos beautiful countryside in the USA, and this guy just wanted it over with. thought to myself, "Well, you paid for this event, why not enjoy it?" I found i odd that someone would choose to pay for an event and then get frustrated abou doing it. Of course, I had no idea what was going on in this person's life tha day. Maybe this man was in pain, or he could have had a personal situation t which he needed to attend that was more important. I remind myself of thi story whenever I feel that I am not being fully present in the moment, whil doing something I should be appreciating.

You might feel testing oneself implies you need to win, but winning ca have a variety of meanings. For example, a few years ago at a bicycle trad show in Las Vegas, I was speaking with Dr. Allen Lim, an author, former che for professional cycling teams, and founder of Skratch nutritional products. was telling him about some challenges a family member had a while back an how well that person was doing now. Dr. Lim responded to my story with thes five words: "Life is about the comebacks." I found his comment to be profoun because it undercuts the proverbial idea that winning is everything. It resonate with me because I think it is so true.

Dr. Lim's statement is very close to this quote, which I believe is attributed to Booker T. Washington: "Success is to be measured not so much by the position that one has reached in life as by the obstacles which he has overcome." As I reflect on the people I have written about in this book and others I know and respect, I realize that many of them have overcome real adversity to win in the end. They dealt with their challenges and turned lemons into lemonade. If you are like me, I almost always root for the underdog. I find joy in watching people and teams exceed expectations. Being around the cycling community has provided many opportunities to watch comebacks and people overcoming obstacles.

SAYING YES TO NEW ADVENTURES

Getting into cycling is also a great way to unearth new adventures and get myself to tackle new exploits. The older I have gotten, the more comfortable I am doing something I have never done before, or doing something I felt I could not do well. In the past, I would not dance, sing, or try something at which I felt I would not excel. I would say no to new ventures, even though I had no idea to what I was saying no.

My new passion for cyclo-cross racing is a prime example of me breaking out of this restrictive habit. "What is cyclo-cross?", you may ask. Imagine riding a road bike with very thick tires through a bumpy grassy field, into mud, and up hills so steep one often has to run up the incline pushing or carrying the bike. And for a little more "fun" in the sport, the sadists designing the courses sneak in jumps, ramps, sand, and other obstacles to punish those silly enough to tackle this sport. That's cyclo-cross.

Why would I start this absurd activity at age 60? Why not? Why not say yes to new adventures? Why not have fun trying new adventures? Why not push one's limits for extreme fun? I should add that I usually come in last o very close to last in these races, but, as the saying goes, "Frankly, my dear, don't give damn!" What I care about is having a good time. The bes compliment I get at these races is people saying how much they enjoy seein the enormous grin plastered across my face the entire time. In addition to m hands, arms, legs, and butt hurting after a race, my face also hurts from smilin so much. This is a win for me!

I quoted Wolfgang Puck in the beginning of this chapter. In this saying, h advises us to ask people not about their jobs but about their hobbies. I often pu a little twist on his suggestion and ask strangers this question: "About what ar you passionate?" I feel this query goes much deeper than the somewhat shallov and typical opening line at a cocktail party of asking what someone does for living. It would be wonderful to hear that what people do for a living is th same as their passion, but usually it's not the case. Asking this question usuall results in a deep, rich conversation.

I also like Puck's quote as it reminds us about the importance of embracin hobbies in life. We all need activities we do purely for fun. I have long enjoye painting and I often tell people I paint because it is something I do for mysel only, and over which I have total control. I can paint on one canvas all weeken and then decide to trash it at the end without even showing it to anyone else o asking anyone's permission. This, for me, is a wonderful form of meditation.

When I pedaled into this love affair with riding bicycles, it opened up a ricl new world of joy and adventure for me. I encourage you to find something t do that you truly love doing. A hobby can be extremely relaxing and a grea form of renewal, self-learning, and meditation. I believe it was Bertrand Russel who said it best: "The time you enjoy wasting is not wasted time." A fantasti saying which, when fully embraced, can provide limitless food for thought.

RECIPE REMINDERS FOR HIGHWAY ONE *DOMESTIQUE*, AND OTHER PEDALING PROVERBS

Find a hobby or activity you do for the pure love of doing it.

If you can volunteer to help a charity, the benefits to you and to others are many.

Do not shy away from sharing experiences with others. Had I not shared the challenges of a family member with Dr. Lim, I would not have heard his words: "Life is about the comebacks."

Remember to say yes to new adventures. Life is too short to be afraid to try new things. And you just might find a new activity you love.

Chapter 15

Disconnecting the Dots

"Just knowing you don't have the answers is a recipe for humility, openness, acceptance, forgiveness, and an eagerness to learn—and those are all good things."

–Dick Van Dyke

Four days after my twelfth Christmas started out like any other wintery school vacation day in our large house on a hill in southeastern Pennsylvania. The quiet stillness and sense of peace that descends on the countryside after freshly fallen snow masked any hint of how, a few hours later, events would unfold to change my life and that of my mother and brother.

My most cherished gift that holiday was the Beatles' *Revolver* album, a prized possession I still have. To this day, I can vividly picture relaxing in the corner of our father's book-lined study, playing my favorite song on the album over and over again on our old record player. As those of you from that generation may remember, back then to play a song over and over you had to gently lift the arm of the record player off the album and place it back down exactly on the groove where the song started.

For reasons I no longer recall, my favorite song on *Revolver* was "Taxman." I must have played it 10 to 15 times in a row, and I had the volume turned up way louder than my father would usually permit. He was toiling away at his big wooden desk about 10 feet behind me, doing some paperwork. I was surprised he didn't tell me to turn down the volume. I felt like I was getting away with something. The beat of the music, the warmth of the room, and m freedom from school—what could be better than that for a 12-year-old?

Over the loud Beatles' music, I heard the creaking of my father's ol wooden chair at his desk as he got up. He walked by me, patted me on the hea without saying a word, and left the room. I didn't think anything of it. I neve saw my father again.

About two hours later, I was in our living room watching television an heard the phone ring on my father's desk. I ran to answer it, expecting it wa one of my friends wanting to go sledding or to play in the neighbor's barn. was disappointed, but not alarmed, when I picked up the heavy black receive and the man on the other end identified himself as Dr. Cottcamp, the local tow physician, who had visited our house several times when I was sick. He aske to speak with our mother. Thinking nothing about why he would be calling, simply yelled to my mother that Dr. Cottcamp was on the phone, and waite for her to pick up in the kitchen. I hung up when I heard her voice on the othe receiver.

Less than three minutes later, my mother came into the living roon sobbing. She called my brother and me together. As we stood there with he hugging us, she informed us that our father had committed suicide. He wa found face-down in an alley in the small town about a mile away from our hom with a gunshot wound to his temple.

The disease of alcoholism had defeated my father. It accomplished it primary mission of killing the person with the disease, while devastating thos impacted by its evil, long-reaching tentacles.

In the following weeks, months, and years, I did what many children unfortunately do in situations like this: I took on responsibility for something I had no rational reason to claim as my own. I connected dots that should never have been connected. I assumed my father's suicide was somehow my fault.

I have read it is not uncommon for children to think they are more responsible for situations than they actually are. They can connect dots where they should not be connected. My connecting the dots between my dad's suicide and me was linked directly to my playing the "Taxman" song that morning and to an innocent comment my mother made a few days later. A stanza of the lyrics of the song are needed to set the stage for understanding why I mistakenly took on this blame for far too many years.

The "Taxman" lyrics include these lines:

"Yeah, I'm the taxman

Don't ask me what I want it for

(Haha, Mr. Wilson)"

The gist of the song is that the taxman will eventually get you. But there is something else in that song you probably did not take note of in the lyrics: the reference to "Mr. Wilson," which is my last name and one I shared with my father.

About three days after my dad's death, my mother was sorting through papers at his desk and announced—having no idea of the consequences a seemingly innocuous statement would have on me—that my father was so thoughtful, he'd completed his taxes that morning before leaving the house and putting a gun to his head. At that instant, this grieving 12-year old boy drew lines between dots that actually never existed. As irrational as it sounds today, as I put this in writing some 40 years later, I assumed my father took his own life because of my playing the "Taxman" song numerous times while he sat behind me working on his taxes, hearing over and over again his name being

called out by The Beatles. This was my deep, dark secret for decades—one tha
I did not feel I could share even with my loving, supportive mother.

Before my father's death, my mother strove to help us manage living wit
an alcoholic parent. She was steadfastly open to discussing the disease c
addiction, which was rare to talk about back then. She gave us unconditiona
love, which went a long way in minimizing the damage of growing up in
family with an alcoholic parent. My brother and I knew our dad had an illnes
and that he went to meetings to try to learn how to stay sober. For reasons I d
not understand, either then or now, and which I now know had nothing to d
with a son he loved, he simply could not beat the disease.

I have come to terms with my father's suicide. Growing up in a home wit
an alcoholic parent has not defined who I am as I refuse to be a victim of pas
circumstances. My life has been full of many wonderful blessings. I ar
thankful for the numerous, varied chapters of my years on this planet—ever
the darker and more challenging ones, as they have resulted in much persona
growth and learning. While my past does not define me, I have studied th
impact growing up with an alcoholic has on children as it is important t
understand the emotional trauma addiction can, and almost always does, hav
on family members.

I believe one can find a silver lining in any of life's events, no matter wha
they are. In this case, I realized I learned a number of positive skills from
childhood such as mine, including resilience, flexibility, independence, and a
keen insight to read people and circumstances. I believe these are traits you wil
often find in adult children of alcoholics.

One of the early pioneers in conducting research on adult children o
alcoholics is Janet Geringer Woititz, whose trailblazing book, *Adult Childrer
of Alcoholics,* I recommend to anyone who wants to learn more on this topic. I
I recall correctly, Ms. Woititz wrote in her book something to the effect of the

ollowing. She stated, tongue in cheek, that it would be useful to ask applicants
1 a job interview if they are an adult child of an alcoholic because their
efinition of a half-day's work is 12 hours. She was clearly being facetious in
1aking this comment, but her point is that children of alcoholics are often very
riven and dedicated to hard work.

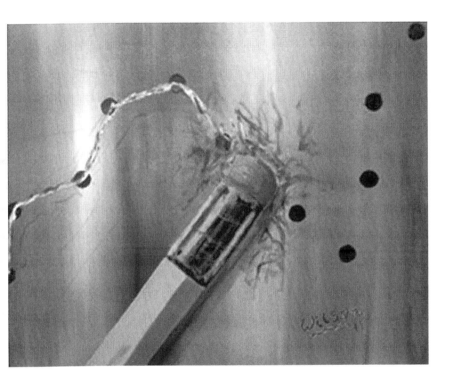

A few years ago I did this painting, titled "Disconnecting the Dots," as I
ontinued to work on my codependency issues. The painting represents for me
he dots I connected relating to my father's suicide. Dots that I never should
ave connected. But more importantly, it also reflects my erasing those dots.
Vhile the lines connecting these dots can never be fully erased, they have
ecome much lighter, both in the art and metaphorically in my emotional
rauma. I have been able to disconnect the dots through a lifetime of hard work

in professional therapy sessions, support groups, and helping others dealing with their loved one's suffering.

As part of my own recovery from codependency, I have attended numerous Nar-Anon (short for Narcotics Anonymous) meetings. These support groups are designed to assist family members and loved ones coping with someone with the disease of addiction. Like AA, this is a 12-step program with the first step being: "We admit we were powerless over the addict—that our lives had become unmanageable." I know that 12-step approaches to recovery may not be for everyone and, in some cases, even the mention of them will turn off readers. Bear with me, though, as I am not going to stand on a soapbox about the benefits of the 12-step approach. I recognize there are several effective ways one can become healthy, both physically and emotionally. Whatever works for someone is a blessing.

Given that, I hope you will read on and allow me to elaborate on what I learned from Nar-Anon's Step One: accepting being powerless over the addict. In embracing this first step, it does not mean accepting you are a victim and are powerless to do anything about a loved one's disease of addiction. Rather, it reminds you simply to live the message of the Serenity Prayer: that we need to accept the things we cannot change, change the things we can, and have the wisdom to know the difference.

As I came to understand the deeper meaning of being powerless over the addict and I applied it to other areas of my life, I no longer felt the need to be the master of the universe over events happening around me. I began to operate with a greater sense of what I had control over versus what I did not. This actually gave me more freedom to have a greater influence over the things I could change. Giving up thinking I had to be totally in charge of everything was very freeing. My entire existence became lighter.

If I have a single message to leave you with, it would be this: For some ings, you do have the power and the reason to connect the dots. For others, s time to disconnect the dots. We need to erase lines we never should have nnected in the first place. Free yourself from the past and live fully in the oment. It is time to cook bagels on your dashboard!

RECIPE REMINDERS FROM DISCONNECTING THE DOTS

Pay close attention to why things happen and be cautious to only accept sponsibility for events you should truly claim as your own.

Share your story with others in an attempt to help them.

Pay close attention to children, especially those dealing with trauma, as they often have a hard time understanding the cause.

The worst thing one can do is to deny or bury emotions from the past. If you are struggling with such issues, please seek professional assistance.

Chapter 16

Lessons from Stolen Peanuts, A Roller Coaster, And Easter Eggs

"I had these recipes that say do this, do that. Who MAKES these rules?"
–Emeril Lagasse

Our cafeteria in elementary school had two vending machines: one for dispensing small cartons of drinks like regular milk, chocolate milk, and orange juice, and one for snacks like potato chips, pretzels, crackers, and peanuts. The snack machine had knobs across the bottom you yanked on, and your selected item would free-fall into a receiving area below. One day, when I was in fourth grade, someone discovered the knob for the bag of peanuts was malfunctioning, dispensing a bag of peanuts every time it was pulled even if no money had been deposited. I bolted over right away and kept pulling the handle until I had filled my gray plastic lunchbox with every single remaining pack of peanuts the machine contained. I was very proud of myself for this accomplishment.

When my mother picked my brother and me up from school that afternoon, I could hardly contain my excitement. Jumping into our 1964 black Ford Falcon with shiny red leather seats, I opened my lunchbox and explained with glee how

I'd gotten my treasure chest of peanuts for free. But, to my surprise, m mother did not have the reaction I expected. I still shudder now, decades late at how livid she was, without even knowing what that word meant at th age. She could not believe what I had done, insisting I had "stolen" th peanuts. She made it crystal clear I would march into the principal's offi the first thing the next morning to apologize and return every bag. I reca trying some lame argument about my crime being justified, given how mar times the machine had ripped me off when I put money in it and got nothin She failed to see the logic of my feeble defense.

Arriving at school the next morning, my mother dragged me to the offi with my ill-begotten loot. With her watching over my shoulder, I did as I wa commanded to do and said I was sorry and returned every bag of peanuts. Th principal was so impressed with my confession, even though I was obviousl making it under duress, that during the morning announcements broadcast ov the public address system to the entire school, he shared the story. He als included my name! While I received compliments from the teachers for m honesty, my peers were not equally impressed. Most of my classmates coul not understand why I had told my mother about this in the first place.

Sadly, whenever I have shared this story with people over the decade many of them say their parents would not have made them return the peanut Rather, they believe their parents would have been proud of them for takin advantage of a malfunctioning vending machine. I have been intrigued with th response and reflected on it for a long time, wondering what values such paren are teaching their children.

Along these lines, I have observed many incidents of parents sendin wrong messages to their children. Since that fateful stolen peanuts day I hav tried to live up to the high ethical standards of my mother, though I know I hav fallen short of them many times when raising my son. So, before calling o ders for their transgressions, I should call myself out first.

One example of my own *faux pas* when I clearly sent the wrong message to my son occurred when he was about ten years old. He was pleading with my wife and me to let him go on a very intense roller coaster in our hometown. The coaster did not have an age limit, just a height limit—all riders had to be over a certain height to get on. My son was at least an inch or two short of the required minimum height. Of course, a proper parenting message would have been to say he needed to wait until he was tall enough. Is that what I did? No. Rather, I found him some platform shoes. So the next weekend he approached the ticket seller with his absurdly added inches. It was not the ticket seller's first rodeo, though, and he practically laughed watching us approach. As our son stood against the wall and put his head next to the required height line, he was still barely tall enough for his head to touch the line. The ticket vendor rolled his eyes, sold us our tickets, and let us pass. We got into our seats, feeling proud we had pulled off our little caper.

However, when the roller coaster started its infamously fast twists and turns, my son started screaming in fear. He was begging me to make it stop. His head and neck flew from side to side as we traversed the sharp curves at God knows how many miles per hour. I told him I could not make the roller coaster stop, but I was so concerned for his well-being I grabbed his head on both sides to keep his fragile neck from snapping. Finally, the terrifying ride came to an end, and neither of us was physically harmed in any way, but I did have a new respect for why roller coasters have a height requirement. I have often thought how devastated I would have been had he gotten injured because I allowed him to cheat the height limit, a rule in place for his own protection! I have also thought about what type of message I sent to our son that day about being acceptable to not respect rules. Clearly, a mistake I regret as a parent.

Over the years, I have observed many parents bending the rules. A comm example is when parents encourage their children to lie about their age to ge less expensive ticket to a movie or other type of event. That lie may seem trivi but I don't think those same parents are too happy when, ten years later, th teen gets a fake ID to buy alcohol or go to bars and clubs! When the paren cannot understand why their teen might do that, they conveniently seem to ha a case of amnesia about the movie ticket scam they perpetrated.

As I wrote this, the get-into-college bribery scandal was hitting t airwaves, revealing how dozens of celebrities and wealthy parents pa exorbitant fees to get their offspring into the most elite schools in the countr These parents literally arranged to cheat on college entrance exams or falsi the athletic prowess of their sons and daughters to ensure admittance to t college of their choice. The children supposedly did not know, but wow! Th is a pathetic example of parents channeling the worst message to children abo the values that should count in life.

I learned many other lessons from my mother about living an ethical lif but I also recall one from my father before he passed on. I was about five or s years old, and we were attending an Easter egg hunt at a stately red bri mansion in the small town where I grew up. As I was scoping out my East egg plan of attack, I discovered a very large yard on one side of the hou overflowing with brightly colored eggs. When the organizer said, "Go," all n competitors went around the house to the other side. No one told us we had go that way so, being creative, I scurried directly to the large open yard and ha free rein to pick up all the eggs I could fit into my basket. At the end of th hunt, my basket was overflowing and I even had eggs crammed into n pockets.

When all the children gathered back together several were in tears, n having stumbled upon any eggs. Noticing how my basket was overflowing, n ther made me share my hard-earned eggs with the kids who were not so lucky. was livid! Through my tears, I protested how unfair it was that I had to share y eggs. I recall protesting that it was not my problem those other kids were ot inventive enough to go the other direction at the start.

Being totally honest here: while I am sure I learned a good lesson about the alue of sharing from my father during this traumatic event, I still have hard eelings about this event. I guess even good lessons are hard to swallow at mes. If this happened today, I might be screaming about the ills of socialism nd how I don't want to share!

Children learn from their parents in many ways. They watch what you do nd how you act. You teach values in everything you do. Many of these lessons learned did not involve my parents saying anything; rather, they were bservational in nature. I recall as a very young boy going with my mother henever she volunteered at Head Start, Planned Parenthood, and several other onprofit organizations. I have many memories of being taken to civil rights narches and other events in the name of justice. Now that I understand one of ne best ways to learn is experiential, I have a great appreciation for my nother's passion for social change and volunteering to help others.

The moral of this essay is timeless, and I hope everyone can agree. Our oal as parents and adults is to pass on to the generation after us the universal esponsibility we all share to live an ethical life. We each have to make choices very day to be honest, tell the truth and not lie, and to honor the ethical choices nat others make.

Living an ethical life can be challenging, I admit. We can often be motional and find ways to justify our actions that are less than honest or ruthful. That said, the optimist in me believes that for the majority of people ur sense of right and wrong is grounded in sound moral principles that, more ften than not, result in our choice to operate within accepted ethical standards and sanctioned laws.

While the above may sound obvious and an easy rule of thumb to follow, admit I fall short of always abiding by rules and laws. I speed when I think my judgment about a safe amount of foot pressure on the gas pedal is wiser than whoever randomly decided what number to print on the signs I am passing. Interestingly, at the same time, I get furious at drivers who decide their own "safe" rate of speed is much faster than what I arbitrarily feel is a safe rate. And while 90% of the time I will tell a waitress or waiter if they left a drink or dessert off my food bill, if the service was poor I might just conveniently "forget" to do so. As I trust is true with many reading this, I plead guilty to situational ethics at times. I know this can have negative consequences, as I have seen too many defendants stand before a judge trying to justify why a certain law did not apply to them or was unfair. These objections are usually made right before they are carted off to jail. Don't be that unfortunate person.

In the end, I think the best we can hope for is a society that aims to be increasingly ethical and honest. We must move in a direction that takes us more towards right than wrong. Adults and parents play a key role in modeling this for each successive generation. I therefore thank my mother for making me return the peanuts and my father for insisting I share the Easter eggs. I am who I am today because of these experiences.

RECIPE REMINDERS FOR LESSONS FROM STOLEN PEANUTS, A ROLLER COASTER, AND EASTER EGGS

- Set a good example for your children and for other children—both in your words and actions.

- Life is much easier if you strive to be honest and forthright, as you do not need to remember what you said to whom, your level of guilt and remorse will be minimal, and you will sleep better at night.

Take time to think about the decisions you make and the impact of those decisions on others.

Chapter 17

"I Have Never Been to Aspen," And Other Job-Hunting Dos and Don'ts

"Cooking is not a science but an art, mistakes are okay, messes are fine—
the pleasure is in the creating and the sharing of the result."
—Lori Pollan, *The Pollan Family Table: The Best Recipes and Kitchen*
Wisdom for Delicious, Healthy Family Meals

What is the best mistake someone else made that benefited you? Mine is undoubtedly how I obtained my first professional job. After earning my Masters of Science degree in Judicial Administration from the University of Denver College of Law, I returned to Pennsylvania to stay close to home as my mother was living alone there. I spent nine months sleeping in my childhood bedroom, working odd jobs while on my quest to secure employment in my desired field. Unfortunately, despite sending out dozens of resumes, I had no success finding a job close to home. At that point, I expanded my job search to look anywhere in the country.

This was back before the Internet, so it was not as easy to search available jobs in other states as it is today. I recall subscribing to a professional monthly newsletter for court administrators that listed job openings. Through this newsletter I saw an announcement for a position in Phoenix with the state trial court. Just as I had done for at least 50 other positions, I mailed a cover lett[er] and resume to the court in Phoenix applying for this position. A few wee[ks] later, I received a call from the court administrator there offering me t[he] position. He informed me to be there to start work in one week. I had not ev[er] interviewed for the job or had any previous contact from anyone in that cou[rt] about the opening!

Despite the strangeness of it, I was in no position to question his decisio[n] making as to why they hired me. I was hungry for an opportunity in my chos[en] profession, so I immediately accepted. With just one week to move across t[he] country, I said my farewells to my mother, packed everything I owned into m[y] little bright yellow 1976 Honda Civic, and started the three-day trek fro[m] Pennsylvania to Arizona. I recall how odd it felt walking into the office for t[he] first time to meet a new boss whom I had never met, but all went well an[d] quickly settled into my new responsibilities.

Approximately three years later I was in my boss's office while he w[as] giving an extern, who was leaving us to attend graduate school, a lecture [on] how to write a resume and how to interview for a new position. This prompt[ed] me to reflect upon my "no interview" hiring, so I asked the court administrat[or] why he had offered me the position. I reminded him how I had sent my resum[e] and then he had called and offered me the job without even interviewing me.

My boss responded by saying, "I knew I wanted to hire you after we spe[nt] that afternoon talking as we sat by the pool at the hotel in Aspen, Colorado." [I] looked at him with a confused expression on my face, and told him, "I hav[e] never been to Aspen." His mouth fell open as he said in a loud and astounde[d] voice: "I hired the wrong damn person!" This is an absolute true story abo[ut] how I got my first break into the field of court administration.

We spent the next few minutes arguing about whether I had ever been [in] Aspen, with my boss insisting that is where he met me. From then on, ever[y] ne the subject would come up, I would remind him I would not have forgotten ending time in Aspen. I often wondered about the poor guy who spent an ernoon sitting by the pool in Aspen with my former boss, impressing him th his skills and credentials, only to not get the job after all! If you are out ere reading this story, my apologies for taking your position in Phoenix all ose years ago.

My message from this story to anyone out there looking for a new career portunity is to apply for any job you want, as they might think you are meone else and hire you by mistake. This is clearly the best mistake that ever ppened to me.

Since then, I have had 35+ years of experience reviewing job applications d interviewing people for various positions. Many of these proved to be teresting experiences—some positive, some not so positive—worthy of aring with anyone entering the job market or considering applying for a new sition. So, here are a few short "Dos and Don'ts Recipes for Job Hunters":

<u>DO</u>

1. Do Your Homework. When I am conducting interviews, I like to ask is question: "You are applying for a job with [insert company name here], so ill you please tell us what you know about us as an employer?" I still remain tounded at how many "deer in the headlights" looks I receive after asking this uestion, with so many people almost completely ignorant about what the job tails. I cannot fathom why someone would apply for a job and not try their est to gain a thorough understanding of the company for which they think they ant to work. On the other hand, I was always very impressed when someone ould respond by citing items from the organization's website and list specific etails they learned about the company. This showed true seriousness about anting to comprehend the job for which they were applying.

Doing my homework paid off early in my career when I was applying for my first position as a Clerk of Court in the field of Court Administration which was my ultimate career goal. I had to interview for this position before panel of seven federal judges, so I read about each one prior to the interview. Fortunately, this court placed a name card on the table in front of each judge I knew who was who during this rather stressful process.

I was only 33 years old at the time—relatively young for this type of senior level opening. Despite the fact that asking someone's age is not an appropriate question in a job interview, I anticipated someone violating that prohibition. Fortunately, the judge who ended up asking me my age was a man who, as I had learned beforehand, was appointed to his lifetime tenured position some years previously when he was only 38 years old! Being appointed that young as a federal judge back then was extremely rare.

The judge queried me: "I know I am not supposed to ask this, but how old are you?" I figured at my relatively young age, interviewing for my ultimate career position, I had nothing to lose so I decided to be a bit more assertive than may have been wise, and I responded with this: "Judge, I am 33 years old, five years younger than you were when you were appointed as a federal judge." I grinned, and the interview moved on to other topics. I was fortunate to obtain this position and, after starting this new job, the judge who had asked my age informed me that one of the reasons I got his vote of approval for the job was I showed I had done my homework and I was not afraid to "give it back to him."

2. Practice. If you are preparing for an interview for a new job, after having been in your current position for a long time, I recommend you set up a practice interview panel with some friends or professional colleagues. This is not different than if you were preparing for a golf tournament or a basketball game and had not played for a while. You'd probably go and hit a few buckets of golf balls at a driving range or shoot some hoops for a few hours to practice your row, right? It's just common sense. Oddly, I have seen many people go into these job interviews who seem to have never practiced. They hesitate and come up blank when asked a fairly simple question.

I strongly encourage you to take the time to practice. It is not that hard. Merely contact a handful of friends, explain the job for which you are applying, ask them to develop a few questions, and set up a time to meet with them for a mock interview. And, very importantly, ask them to critique you after the session.

3. Be Aware of Your Eye Contact. I have seen many applicants blow an interview by focusing their eye contact and responses only on the person they think will be making the ultimate decision. Or, more disturbing, they give male members on the interviewing panel eye contact while ignoring the female panel members. I cannot recall ever hiring someone after they displayed this disturbing use of eye contact. That said, an interviewer needs to be cognizant that some cultures have different norms when it comes to the use of eye contact.

4. Have a Strong Closing. Often, at the end of an interview, the interviewers will ask if the applicant has any questions or final thoughts they want to share. Regarding questions, if you have any legitimate ones about the position, this is the time to ask. However, I suggest you not ask something like this: "How did I do in the interview?" or "What are the traits you are looking for in the successful candidate?" I have had many applicants ask questions along these lines, and I do not believe they are appropriate. Your goal in interviewing is to be offered the position, not to ask for feedback or for advice on traits you should possess for the position.

I also advise job candidates to remember you are interviewing the new prospective employer as well. So, when thinking about questions to ask at the end of the interview, I believe it is fine to ask questions about the position if they are important considerations for you before accepting an offer. For example, if having authority over a certain aspect of the job is a "make or break" factor for you, asking about this is acceptable. But I would start such a question with a statement like this: "As I am sure you want the new hire to be a win/win for your company and the individual, it is important to me to understand if the position will have authority over [whatever the topic is]?" However, given my previous admonition about asking the wrong questions, an alternative strategy is to save such a question for the next step in the process once you are offered the position. There is no hard and fast approach to questions like this, but depends on the interview and you need to assess the situation. My bottom line is to encourage you to think thoroughly through these questions so you are well prepared for the interview.

Your final closing remarks are important to leave the interviewer(s) on positive note. I suggest you make it clear you want the position. This is not the time to be timid; highlight why you believe you are the best person for the job. You should be, of course, tactful and not boastful, but it is good to tell the interviewer(s) why you believe their organization needs you. Coupling your strong closing with some humility, i.e., recognizing you would have some areas to learn to become the best employee in the organization, goes a long way as well to impress the decision makers.

DON'TS

The following recommendations of things not to do may seem outrageously silly to mention, but I have experienced all of these when doing interviews or screening applicants. No commentary is necessary. Just don't do these.

1. Don't come to interview without washing your hands—especially if you just cut the grass and your hands smell like gasoline.

2. Do not put your feet up on the table during the interview.

Do not sign your cover letter for a position as a United States Magistrate Judge (or for any other position) with a purple crayon.

Do not hand out business cards to the female members on the interview panel promoting the beauty products you sell on the side.

RECIPE REMINDERS FOR "I HAVE NEVER BEEN TO ASPEN," AND OTHER JOB HUNTING DO'S AND DON'TS

Do your homework when applying for positions and do not be afraid to go for a job even if you do not think you have a chance, as they might think you are someone else!

Know your audience in a job interview.

The goal of the interview is to get to the next step, not to negotiate fine points about the position; those discussions are best held for after you get an offer.

Be confident, be genuine, and enjoy the experience.

Chapter 18

Elvis Lives In Las Vegas (And saved the day at a church event!)

"The thing with food is that you can give 20 people the same recipe and the same ingredients, and somebody's going to make it better than somebody else, and that's the creativity of it. It's like music. You could have a bunch of people playing the same piece, and somebody's gonna play it better."

–Dweezil Zappa

Picture standing in a long line on a sidewalk in Las Vegas in the middle of July around noon. There is no shade. There is no relief from the blazing sun, a sun which makes your skin feel like it is melting after just a few minutes. Now also picture yourself being elderly in this long line of about 150 people. You require a walker or a cane to stay upright. Or, possibly you are in a wheelchair. This mass of people consists of people of all ages, with only a small percentage sharing your health challenges. You are waiting to get inside the doors of a church for a buffet lunch being provided at the weekend conference you are attending. The line is moving, but very slowly.

As you inch closer to the doors, getting somewhat weak from being exposed to the extreme heat, a tall, thin, figure appears with jet black hair poofed up in a wave on his head. This man is well over six feet tall and is

119

wearing a glitter-studded white jumpsuit. To use a term you have heard from your grandchildren, he is all blinged out. You worry you may be hallucinating. You wipe sweat from your eyes and, lo and behold, standing before you is Elvis Presley! Now you are pretty sure you are having a flashback. But then Elvis touches your arm and softly whispers in your ear: "Come with me." It seems way too real to be a mirage. He escorts you past the younger people standing line, opens the door, and leads you to the food. Just as he appeared out of nowhere to guide you to the air conditioning, he disappears back into the crowd.

Unbeknownst to you, Elvis has gone back outside to guide other elderly conference attendees to the front of the line to get them out of the heat. He continues on this quest. Arm in arm, he guides several elderly men and women into the cool sanctuary. While performing this act of kindness, Elvis is very polite—and even apologetic—to the others standing in line as he kindly informs them he is leading these people inside the building for their own safety. No one objects to Elvis being the knight in shining armor—or, I should say, the knight in the sequin diamond-studded jumpsuit.

No, the above story was not a mirage from the heat of the desert. I observed Elvis doing this at a church conference I was largely responsible for organizing. This weekend retreat brought pastors and other church leaders from several congregations in Southern California to Las Vegas. We hired a local Elvis impersonator to give a bit of Las Vegas flare over the lunch hour.

While I will continue to refer to this amazing man as "Elvis," I want to give credit where it is truly deserved. "Elvis" was in fact Eddie Powers, a long-time and highly respected Elvis impersonator. Given Mr. Powers' highly entertaining appearance at this meeting and him going above and beyond by helping the elderly attendees, I agree with the name of his website BestElvisInVegas.com.

Here are the two main "food for thought" lessons I learned from Elvis that day. Of course the first message, the obvious one, was Elvis's act of kindness. Anytime anyone exhibits acts of kindness, they deserve a thank you and recognition. So, Eddie Powers, AKA Elvis: thank you! Elvis saw a problem and jumped in to solve it, without being asked or asking permission to do so. He just instinctively knew the right thing to do and did it.

My second takeaway I am not so proud to share, but need to because it is equally important. I was in the same line and did not recognize the need to give the elderly attendees this level of compassion and care. And, keep in mind: the line consisted largely of pastors from other churches. None of them took action, either. Rather, it took a paid entertainer to do what all of us should have done. A person who was there for a couple hours to entertain stepped up when others stood by idly, oblivious to the obvious need. As I am a firm believer that we learn from our mistakes, I have tried very hard to be more aware of others' needs ever since Elvis swooped in and saved the day that sweltering day outside that church.

As Dweezil Zappa said in the opening quote: "You could have a bunch of people playing the same piece, and somebody's gonna play it better." We had a bunch of people standing in the same line, and Elvis played it better.

RECIPE REMINDERS FROM ELVIS LIVES IN LAS VEGAS (AND SAVED THE DAY AT A CHURCH EVENT!)

- Pay attention to those around you, especially the elderly or others in need, and take action to improve the situation whenever needed.

- We can, and do, learn from all around us if we are truly open to learning.

- Don't wait to ask permission if you see someone in need and you can do something about it.

- And, it seems fitting to close with a line from Elvis's song *A Little Le Conversation*: "A little less fight and a little more spark, close your mouth ar open your heart."

STATEMENT FROM EDDIE POWERS, AKA ELVIS

I distinctly remember thinking if I was their age I would really like to ge out of the extreme heat and through those doors as fast as possible, no matte what it took. So that's what I did that day. I took one or two or three of them however many there were, and brought them through the doors into the front of the line inside the building. I just could not bear to think of them standing ou there in that heat. I had to do something and not just observe that scene and d nothing. I am very touched Lance Wilson remembered this story so many yea later, and am honored to have this shared in his book.

Chapter 19

First and Last Blind Date

"If there is a recipe for success in life, it starts with picking the right
ingredients."
–Anonymous

ave you ever been on a blind date? If so, how did it work out? I was only on one blind date in my life, and saying yes to this request from a friend rned out to be the best decision of my life. This is when I laid my eyes upon e beautiful and amazing Joy Seward—now Joy Wilson. I know that as the ader you cannot see me sitting here at the computer, struggling mightily with ow to proceed after those opening sentences. The other chapters were easier write. How do I begin to paint a picture of someone who has brought me nconditional love and support for almost half my life? How do I condense most 30 years of life-changing experiences into one chapter? Sitting here, aring at the half page of text once again with a bad case of writer's block, I k myself what to include. What will not fit? Okay, just write. Just write and e what happens. Type. Let the words flow. Then edit at the end.

After much free flow typing, deleting, and starting over (maybe I should ave let all the editing appear in this final version?), I decided to focus on just ne of the many values I learned from my life partner: compassion. And while

I could tell endless stories about Joy's compassionate nature, I will limit this three areas: caring for strangers, feeding the homeless, and pet therapy.

Unlike me, Joy is an extrovert. So, when I mention her caring for strangers I should replace the word "stranger" with "a friend she has not met yet." Joy can enter a convenience store for two minutes and walk out having made a new friend. She now knows the new friend's name, number of kids, hobbies, and health challenges. How does that happen? Being an introvert, I have no idea but I love that about her. A more concrete example of Joy caring for strangers occurred shortly after her mother entered a memory care unit. After visiting few weeks, Joy knew all the other resident's names and interacted with them as much as she did with her own mother. And, of course, she also knew the employees by name. Treating everyone with respect and dignity is just part of her nature. It comes naturally for her.

As for feeding the homeless, she keeps both our cars stocked with packs of crackers; each one with a dollar bill rubber-banded around it. We give these to homeless people on the street corners. I understand the objections to this form of giving, i.e. that we should be giving the money to a charity instead, as the homeless person may use the dollar for drugs or alcohol. Yes, that is possible. But, for Joy, it comes down to this simple statement: if they need to stand on the corner and ask for money or food, they need it more than she does. No rules. No judgment. Very simple.

She also brought this sense of compassion to a local food bank she started several years ago. It was open twice a month and quickly was feeding hundreds of families. While some food banks limited the number of times a person could come, or had some other restrictions, Joy's approach was similar to helping those on our street corners: whoever showed up got food. She was the director of this food bank for five years when she had to stop for health reasons. And her decision to stop was one of the few times, if not the only time, that I put my

ot down and insisted she stop. No, not because I did not want her to continue
is much needed outreach. Rather, due to her health challenges, she paid a
ige physical price every week from packing a trailer with cases of food,
loading the trailer, stocking shelves, and filling bags with groceries. She was
so much pain I insisted she reduce her hours or stop. She reluctantly agreed.
ut, showing the traits of a good leader, she made sure a very dedicated person
ok charge before relinquishing her duties. The food bank continued long after
ie moved on to other adventures.

I am not sure what Joy loves more, dogs or me. That probably depends on
e day and what mischief I got into. She found an inspiring means of turning
er love for dogs into a social outreach program through pet therapy. We have
id several dogs, and she always takes the steps required to get them certified
; therapy dogs. Joy and our dogs have done many different pet therapy
ctivities, including visiting the elderly in nursing homes, spending time with
I children in the hospital, and having our dogs sit with young reluctant readers
; they read to the dog. This last activity builds the child's confidence level
ith reading, as the dog does not judge their abilities. Wouldn't we all benefit
om having someone sit quietly next to us, supporting our every effort with no
idgment?

Joy's most recent job with our dog is visiting three different foster care
icilities so the young children can learn skills while playing with and taking
ire of the dog. These outings are always a win-win for the dog, for her, and
ir the children. The children play fetch with the dog, groom her, and walk her
uring each visit. One of the foster care children said, with a look of wonder
hile walking our dog that he had never walked a dog before! He was beaming,
ie dog's tail was wagging, and Joy was holding back tears of joy (pun
itended). Yes, these outings are truly a win-win for all involved!

I opened this chapter with this quote: "If there is a recipe for success in li⌐ it starts with picking the right ingredients." In no way do I mean to say Joy an "ingredient," although I have undoubtedly said more awkward things in o⌐ many years together. Nor do I claim to have "picked" her, as it was more like⌐ the other way around. Rather, I used this quote because we make choices eve⌐ day about the people with whom we will surround ourselves. We ma⌐ decisions about with whom we spend time and selections about our close circ⌐ of friends. I am convinced making good choices along these lines great⌐ impacts our success and happiness in life. I am blessed to have such compassionate, caring life partner. Joy truly is the perfect life ingredient!

I remain thankful I said yes when asked if I wanted to meet Joy through⌐ blind date. I remain thankful for the numerous lessons she has taught me abo⌐ compassion, caring for strangers, and selflessness. This book would not ha⌐ been possible without her encouragement, support, and unconditional love.

RECIPE REMINDERS FOR FIRST AND LAST BLIND DATE

- Say yes to new adventures, even if it means taking a risk.
- Helping those less fortunate than ourselves is one of our life callings and a very rewarding endeavor.
- Sharing one's life with another person can be a wonderfully rewarding ar⌐ life-changing experience.

Conclusion

contemplated writing a final chapter summarizing the main points of each chapter. After giving that idea more thought, I decided having you draw ur own conclusions was a more interesting approach. So, here is a space for u to do just that:

RAW YOUR OWN CONCLUSIONS

Or, if you prefer, write your own summary:

_____

_____

_____

_____

_____

_____

_____

Either way, I would greatly appreciate it if you would share your conclusions with me.   You can do so by e-mailing them to me dashboardbagels@gmail.com.

Thank you!

Acknowledgments

Dashboard Bagels would not have been possible without the fantastic assistance of several people. Starting with the most significant, my spouse, Joy Wilson. Her unwavering support and encouragement provided me with the energy and commitment to complete this endeavor. She also read and reread the numerous drafts of this book so many times she undoubtedly knows these stories by heart!

Deep gratitude is also extended to Rick Benzel who served as my primary editor. I would send Rick a rough draft of a chapter and it always came back vastly improved. And, while he had a green light to do extensive line editing, he ensured that my voice still told each story. If you are contemplating writing a book, I encourage you to consider him as your editor. You can learn more about his services at rickbenzel.com.

Thanks is also extended to the Honorable Nancy L. Allf, who also read several chapters and gave me valuable recommendations and insights. And a few others, who opted to remain anonymous, provided editorial comments – thank you – you know who you are!

I also want to thank my long-time friend, Brian Swanson at brianswansonstudio.com for his brilliant cover design and excellent work in laying out this book and getting it prepared for printing. Brian's attention to detail is unsurpassed. He went above and beyond in providing insightful suggestions, catching mistakes I missed, and in getting this in the proper format for printing. Thank you, Brian!

Finally, thanks to all those who provided inspiration for *Dashboard Bagels: Dishing Up Food for Thought* through your curiosity, resilience, perseverance, and wisdom. These stories are a tribute to the positive influence you have had on many individuals and on the world.

Made in the USA
Columbia, SC
02 November 2020

23839955R00078